DON'T SWEAT THE
TALK
STUFF

Instant Help
for Nervous Speakers

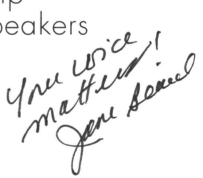

AVIVA
PUBLISHING
New York

Jane Beard

No problem can be solved from the
same level of consciousness
that created it.

— **Albert Einstein**

InVisible Light, Inc.

DON'T SWEAT THE TALK STUFF!
Instant Help for Nervous Speakers

www.InVisibleLight.com

Editor: Tyler Tichelaar
Cover & Interior design by: FusionCW.com

Published by:
Aviva Publishing
Lake Placid, NY
518-523-1320
www.avivapubs.com

Address all inquiries to:
support@InVisibleLight.com

ISBN: 978-1-938686-75-7

Library of Congress Control Number: 2013946155

Disclaimer

The material contained in this book was developed from the personal and professional experiences of the author, Jane Beard. Ms. Beard is not a mental health professional and makes no claim to be one. She does not make any diagnoses, and she makes no claims to be able to do so.

This book is not intended as a substitute for the advice of and treatment by a qualified physical or mental health professional. The publisher and author are not responsible for any adverse consequences or experiences that may result from the use of the ideas, perspectives, and/or tools discussed in this book.

If you proceed to read and use the material contained in this book, you are accepting responsibility for your actions and the results you create. If you have questions about the efficacy and utility of this material for you, we advise you to consult a health professional or other qualified advisor before implementing the ideas shared here.

To Jeffrey B. Davis

My perfect partner in life, love, work, and baseball rooting.

Acknowledgements

I am indebted to the clients, from all around the world, who have trusted me to help them past fear of performance anxiety and stage fright. Without exception, they are people who have true gifts to share with the world.

Some have insights and business acumen that have transformed the companies, businesses, or teams they lead. They decided to stop living with anxiety and dissolve it, so they'd finally have freedom to speak and lead. It was a gift to me to help them get there.

Others have artistic skills that delight audiences of all types. Some were starting out careers, while others were already boldface names in People magazine. All of them reached a new level of freedom and resilience in performance that directly impacted their audiences.

I thank them all profoundly:

My husband of twenty-five years, Jeffrey B. Davis, who has loved and supported me for so long. That he's also my business partner is a gift on top of a gift.

Kim Schraf, for reading the manuscript and giving me such wise feedback.

My friends Naomi Jacobson and Kathryn Klvana, who along with Kim form the members of the Coven, for a safe space for growth and exploration (and champagne).

Annie Groeber, my friend who makes me laugh more than almost anyone else, for encouraging this project for all the years it took finally to make it manifest.

Meredith Self, my soul sister—so much of who I am now is due to your love and insight and example and friendship.

Sandra Mayo, who first taught me about "Subby." Also, Tapas Fleming, Dr. Larry Nims, and so many practitioners in the realm of energy psychology who helped me learn and grow.

Dot Newman and Leslie Jacobson, who directed me before, during, and after my own bouts of stage fright, for your support, encouragement, and love in action.

Jerry Whiddon, who ran the Round House Theatre for many years and taught me the best of what I know about performing. And Marty Lodge and Kathryn Kelley, my long-time acting partners, who challenged and pushed me to experience the exhilaration of trusting the present moment on stage, no matter what. And Jean Whiddon, for the title.

And my kids: Lee, Adrian, Owen, and Lindsay. I am so much richer for having you in my life.

Table of Content

Chapter
One

There's More To Stage Fright Than You Think

They say that the fear of public speaking is greater, for many people, than the fear of death. I think that's an exaggeration. But if you're reading this, it might not feel like much of an exaggeration.

Maybe you have a presentation looming around the corner—today, tomorrow, next week. And you're somewhere along the spectrum from mildly anxious to seriously intimidated.

You've lived with stage fright and speaker anxiety—I'll use the terms interchangeably here—for a long time now.

It's been there, at a low level, probably even before you started to notice it. Long before it started to interfere with your work life, or your capacity to speak up for your kids at the PTA meeting, or sing in church—or all the other places that speaker anxiety can rear its ugly head—it was there. As you started to notice it, it started to get worse, right? And then you'd get more nervous about noticing it, and the more you noticed it, the worse it got.

That is…unless you're one of the people who was fine one day and then: boom! Full blown stage fright out of nowhere.

You may be someone who grits her teeth and lives through each speaking requirement hoping to come out whole on the other end. Or you may be someone who actively ducks all occasions to speak in public.

You may seek help because you finally want to get promoted into a new position, but confident speaking is required to be considered a viable candidate. You may want help because you're sick of losing sleep worrying about speaking in front of a room full of live humans.

However you came by it, however long it's been with you, no matter how acute the anxiety is, I want to help you dissolve it and put it in the past. I want to see you stand in the spotlight and own your voice, your ideas, so you're seen and heard.

My company, Invisible Light (www.InVisibleLight.com), owned by my husband Jeff Davis and me, offers all kinds of help for scared speakers. We coach them one-on-one. We bring workshops to entire departments at some companies—because one of the sneaky little facts about stage fright is this:

Lots of people have speaker anxiety, even if they don't look like they do.

Here's how we know this. When I go to a company to give a workshop on business presentations in the age of Twitter, I ask questions of the participants before I begin. I used to ask, "Who has speaker anxiety?" out loud, right in front of everybody. And I was surprised that so few people would raise their hands.

Then I started to ask people privately, before they arrived at the workshop, "Do you get anxious before presentations? Does that anxiety interfere with the job you wish you could do?"

And always, more than half the participants say, "Yes." But ask them in public, and almost no one cops to it.

So right away, know this: You aren't alone. In fact, you're in the majority. Even some people who LOVE public speaking can get anxiety bad enough to interfere with the job they want to do in front of an audience.

Here's the next thing I want you to know about you and your stage fright:

You are braver than you realize.

You aren't hiding out anymore, gutting it out alone. You're not pretending that it's no big deal to you. Just by reading this book, you're taking steps to find out how to step into yourself and find your voice...steps to put your ideas, your vision, yourself in the spotlight so others can benefit from what you know, what you do, and how you see the world.

You're making yourself vulnerable, so you can become stronger. I honor that, and I know how hard it is.

Because I was once like you.

In the mid-1980s, I had stage fright so bad that I had to quit my job for 2 ½ years. Which was a problem, because I was an actor.

I was in a hit play at the time. The production was *A Coupla White Chicks Talking*, produced in a theatre in Washington D.C. There was only one other actor in the play, and she was a dear friend. We were scheduled to run four weeks.

We kept selling out…so the run kept being extended. Each time the producers extended the run, I got more nervous. It was no big deal at first. I just noticed I was more anxious than usual. Then I started messing up lines here and there. One night, I broke a coffee cup on stage by mistake and I just froze. Things went downhill fast.

Soon, I wasn't sleeping well. I dreaded going to the theatre at night. And so when the producers came to ask for one final two-week extension, I lied to them. I said, "Oh, I'm sorry! I have this trip coming up and I can't change it." And then I *did* go out of town. All because I was too ashamed to tell the truth:

I was a nervous wreck, and the nerves were taking over even outside the theatre.

I bet you've done something similar—ducked out of a request or a demand to speak somewhere. Maybe played it off that someone else should do it, or that you were too busy.

It doesn't feel good, does it? I know for a fact it doesn't.

For those 2 ½ years, I couldn't act. At one point, I got so nervous that I couldn't be in a theatre to watch a play I wasn't even in. A few minutes before curtain, my heart would be racing, my palms would be sweating, and I'd have a tough time breathing. Pretty inconvenient for an actor.

I needed help. I looked lots of places, but there was no Google then, and I didn't find anything that worked. I read books. I went to therapy. It turned out I was looking for someone like present-day me to help, but I found no one. I feel bad for the *me* I was then! I wish so much I could have found someone then who knew what I'm going to clue you into here.

I loved acting and I missed doing it, so I was ashamed of myself for faltering. I called myself every name in the book...probably like you do.

Then I stumbled on the big secret about stage fright—something so powerful it started to change everything.

It's something no one ever tells you, either. They tell you the DUMB stuff: "Think of the audience members in their underwear. Have a glass of wine. Pretend they aren't there. Tell yourself to suck it up; get over it." You know it's dumb because you've heard it over and over, too—you may even have tried it, and you found out it doesn't work.

Once I found the secret, and I figured out how it applied to me, everything changed. Eventually, I went back to work and made a nice, six-figure living as an actor for years.

But even when stage fright was no longer my struggle, I saw its impact all the time. I saw other actors struggle with it, even successful ones.

In the meantime, people started asking me to coach business executives, to show them what I know about deliberate, authentic performance. Soon I spotted them struggling with it. I saw executives who were so smart, so visionary—and too afraid to speak what they knew from a stage, or from the front of a meeting room.

I saw people, a lot of them women, just STUCK at a career level they should have gone beyond. But because they couldn't speak with confidence, they'd never been promoted. I saw talented young actors who were great until they got in a high stakes audition, and then they'd just shut down, and the director would never see the talent that was in them. I'd see friends who were really successful performers, name brand people you see in *People* magazine, suddenly wrestling with this demon.

That's when I realized:

It doesn't matter how successful you are. Stage fright can happen to people at all levels, in all walks of life.

So I started to study and look for more clues to help me understand why it was happening and how I could help. From the world of brain science, I learned amazing facts about how smart our brains are, and how our body, mind, and spirit work together in astounding ways.

From the realm of energy psychology and emotional neuroplasticity, I learned awesome techniques that seem to transform the way people think, feel, and act—even with long-standing issues that have caused them harm or distress for an extended time.

From the realm of Chinese medicine, acupuncture, and energy medicine, I learned other tools that help transform situations on physical and emotional levels.

From the realm of mindful meditation, I learned how to be conscious of, and okay despite, conflicting emotion.

The more I learned, the more I realized that I could help people with stage fright. I discovered there were different *kinds* of stage fright, and you couldn't attack them all the same way.

I developed a six-step process to D-Solve Stage Fright Now™, and it's brought enormous benefits to so many people. In my work with stage fright sufferers, we:

Demystify the Secret behind Stage Fright
Decode the Fear
Deconstruct the Messages
Dissolve the Triggers
Discover a reliable process for connecting with the audience
And
Deliver speakers into freedom to speak up for their ideas, their businesses, and themselves, in their own authentic voices.

Let's get you started to D-Solve Stage Fright Now™!

Remember:

- You aren't alone—more people have speaker anxiety than you realize.

- You're braver than you realize because you're no longer pretending your anxiety isn't an issue.

- I've been where you are, and how! I've helped so many people put stage fright in the past so they can own the spotlight for their ideas and themselves. You can do it, too.

- All kinds of people get stage fright, including people you'd think were bulletproof.

- You have things to say. People are counting on you to say them. The journey you're beginning isn't just for you....It's for them, too.

Chapter
Two

Demystify the Secret Behind
Stage Fright

The more I learned, the more I saw how powerful the secret behind stage fright really is. Here it is:

Stage fright isn't the problem.

Stage fright is the SOLUTION to an even bigger problem your subconscious mind is trying to avoid.

Now, I know you're probably thinking, "Well, it's a problem for ME!" And I get that it's causing you problems. I get that the impact of stage fright is not something you want to live with anymore. I hear you.

But let's just unpack this a bit more. Stage fright is the solution to an even bigger problem the subconscious mind has spotted and is trying to protect you from.

So the chest-pounding, stomach-turning, mouth-drying symptoms of stage fright or performance anxiety aren't signs that there's something wrong with you. Exactly the opposite! They're signs that your body is doing exactly what it evolved to do: protect you from danger. You're experiencing the **fight, flight, or freeze** syndrome you may have learned about in eighth grade biology.

You may not like the symptoms of anxiety, especially when they progress to some of the more extreme symptoms like shortness of breath, nausea, or hives. But understanding why they're happening—and the ways in which your body is reacting in a totally reasonable way to a threat it perceives as extreme—is a great first step toward resolving the underlying issues that trigger your anxiety in the first place. If nothing else, you can **stop being anxious about being anxious**.

Let's back up, though, and make sure that what you're feeling actually is anxiety, and not anticipation or excitement. In our experience, a remarkable number of people confuse anxiety with anticipation.

Anxiety and anticipation aren't the same thing.

Both sets of emotions are experienced, by most people, in the stomach area. Both can be overwhelming, even though only one is a "negative" emotion. That's just the start of the chain of confusion.

Anxiety generally is experienced as:

- butterflies in the stomach
- pounding heart
- sweaty or tingling palms

- dry mouth

- thought patterns that fall somewhere along the spectrum of "It will be over soon" to "I hope nothing awful happens" to "They'll hate me; I know it" to "There must be some way to get out of this."

- a feeling of cloudy thinking, or being outside your body

- the sensation that your sight and hearing are altered

- nausea, which may or may not include intestinal distress

- light-headedness

- the inability to sleep the night before

- looping thoughts about all the things that can go wrong

Anticipation and excitement often are experienced as:

- butterflies in the stomach that don't feel bad

- your heart starts pounding

- sweaty palms

- thought patterns that fall along the spectrum of, "This will be fun" to "I can't wait to do the part where…" to "They are gonna love this!" to "I might be sorry when this is over."

- the sensation that your sight and hearing are altered

- light-headedness

- the inability to sit still or sleep well the night before

- looping thoughts about how things will go, and how much good feedback you will get afterwards

Did you notice that the "symptoms" of each are almost identical? When we grow up, most people talk about nerves and eagerness as synonymous, so we don't learn to differentiate between the two.

I can't count the number of people we've worked with who have been intensely worried about the sensations in their bodies—only to discover the difference between being eager and being anxious. Finding out they were also eager, not only anxious, was a revelation to them. They had been misinterpreting their reactions as "all" nerves, and then they felt even worse about being "so nervous." Seeing that it can be a mixed bag, of which "anxiety" was only part, made a big difference.

This revelation didn't change what they were feeling. All that changed was their relationship to what they were feeling…and that's huge in itself! In modern society, we believe that anxiety is "bad." So their fear stopped once they stopped misinterpreting their bodies' signals as anxiety and assigned a more positive meaning to their feelings.

So, which camp are you in? Have you properly labeled what you are feeling?

Listen to how you talk to yourself, as you prepare your performance. Are you using only words that indicate you're afraid of what is coming? Are you using language that indicates some eagerness for the event? Or both? Do the butterflies in your stomach feel fun and happy, or do they only feel heavy and noxious? You can use that information to label appropriately whether your "nerves" might be partly anticipation instead of only anxiety.

If you find that you're really experiencing anxiety, keep reading. You need to understand what's happening in your brain and your body.

If you discover what you're feeling is rampaging excitement, keep reading. Too much of anything—even a "positive" energy like anticipation—can get in the way of any performer.

Remember:

Stage fright isn't the problem. It's your subconscious's best solution to a bigger problem.

So we've demystified the secret behind stage fright. Now let's find some ways to work with it.

TRY THIS NOW!

Here's the first tactic you should take away and start using immediately:

Stop telling yourself you aren't nervous. Stop trying to ignore the symptoms of nervousness.

The more you ignore the nervousness, the harder your brain will work to get you to notice it. The harder it works, the more chemicals it dumps, and the worse you feel.

It's a vicious cycle, and you can stop it.

It's easier to do than you think.

When you start to feel nervous, change the habit of telling yourself to snap out of it. Let go of the urge to believe that the nervousness is the problem. Remember that it's warning you about a bigger problem.

When your "check engine" alert lights up your car dashboard, you don't say, "Oh, what a disaster! That light is such a loser! Look at it going on like that! I can't stand that light!" You don't do that at all.

You don't behave as if the light is a problem because you recognize immediately that it's alerting you to a problem that was previously invisible to you. You take action by getting the car to the garage to be checked.

And while you may end up cursing the mechanic for charging so much, you are definitely not cursing the red light just for turning on. You might even be grateful that you got it to the mechanic to avoid even worse damage.

That's what your anxiety is doing: pointing you to pull over and check the engine. Don't get mad at it for that. Don't call it any names. Literally say, "Thank you for alerting me." And watch what happens then: Almost immediately, your body will probably stop working so hard to get your attention.

In the next chapter, we'll look at some more specific tools you can use when the stage fright "check engine" light comes on. But for now, use this one:

Don't ignore the light. And don't diss it either. Your body is working brilliantly to help you. We're just going to help it to help you better.

The second tactic will pay long-term dividends, in a huge way—but it's not a quick fix:

Practice mindfulness.

Mindfulness is a form of meditation you can do anywhere. It can be done sitting, standing, or walking. You can have your eyes closed or open. It doesn't matter whether you start out feeling peaceful, or in full-fledged fight, flight, or freeze mode. It doesn't matter where you end up, either. How you feel is immaterial to the doing of it. It's got roots in Buddhist practice, but it's also a skill taught in huge businesses around the globe.

In fact, Google actually has a series of classes in mindfulness practice because the research is clear: Cultivating mindfulness has great business implications.

Mindfulness is exactly as it sounds: It creates a habit of being open to noticing all that's going on in and around you, and not just the endless mind chatter soundtrack that runs amok in so many brains (mine included).

Research shows that mindfulness changes behavior, and it helps tremendously in the area of emotional resilience in particular. Part of how it works is that it literally changes the brain—neuroplasticity is what that's called—and the pathways on which neurons fire.

At InVisible Light, we highly recommend the book *Search Inside Yourself* by Chade-Meng Tan. He's the teacher in charge of personal development at Google, and a former engineer. It's the best business book we've seen in a while!

Here's a simple mindfulness exercise you can do right now.

Find a resting place to stand or sit. Make sure all your devices are turned off, so you won't be tempted to tweet or check mail for three minutes, which is all this exercise will take.

Rest your hands on your lap or a table, and now place your index finger into the palm of the other hand. You get to pick which index finger, and then rest it in the opposite palm. Notice how you can feel the tip of your finger, and the way it's just resting. See if you notice it getting any heavier. Just notice what you notice.

In a few seconds, when you have a sense that you've found what there is to notice, shift your attention to the palm and the spot where that index finger is resting. Notice how that spot is now alive with feeling while you weren't really aware of it when your attention was all on the index finger. Pretty interesting, huh?

Now see if you can feel the space between the palm and the index finger. Physics tells us that this space is empty, and that the finger isn't literally touching the palm. It doesn't feel that way, does it?

Now deliberately shift your attention between the index finger and the palm. See what you notice.

When you're done, just sit up and return to reading.

One thing I want to point out is that you were highly tuned in to whatever your attention was on. Did you notice how the palm skin would seem to go away when you were focused on the index finger? And yet it was right there all along.

And did you notice how you weren't judging your index finger or your palm? Neither was deficient. Neither was letting you down. You felt one and then the other. You felt the intersection between them. No judgment, no recrimination or "it should be different" about it. Just pure noticing *What Is*.

Mindfulness is great at helping people see What Is, without the story of what it's supposed to be. When you're mindful, you detach your beliefs of how an index finger is supposed to feel in a palm, and you just experience it.

When you're anxious about speaking to a room full of team members, you also can be mindful of what you're feeling. Don't judge it ("I'm in trouble now!"). Try just noticing it: "Yeah, there's that quiver I get in my stomach sometimes. But there's also something else there...what is that?"

The more you practice mindfulness, the more you'll start to develop pathways to noticing without judgment. And before we go farther, let me just directly address those of you who are sitting here saying to yourself: "But *judgment* is how I motivate myself! I need judgment!"

To you I ask: How is that going for you? Is judgment really helping? Do you mean to say you actually would try *not* to do a good job on something if you weren't scolding yourself the whole way to the goal? Really?

I didn't think so. You aren't six anymore—or sixteen. You've outgrown the need to give yourself an inner spanking and be mean to yourself, especially when it comes to stage fright.

Here's something else I want you to notice about the mindfulness exercise you just did.

In you, right now, and all along, is a sense of peace. It exists right alongside your tiredness, your hunger, your excitement, and your anxiety. It doesn't vanish and come back. Your attention on it changes, but *it* never does.

Here's what that implies for handling stage fright. We want you to be mindful of the symptoms of stage fright. We want you to notice them. Notice—not judge. Then shift your attention to a place of peace within you. Don't ask yourself where it is and start hunting. Just intend to notice it, and you'll suddenly feel it. It may be small at first, and it may not be broadcasting a very strong signal. But the more you practice noticing it, the easier it will become to find it.

The easier it gets to find it, the faster you can access it later, even in the midst of a real anxiety attack.

So to recap:

NOW: Stop pretending you aren't nervous. Let it be okay that you are.

Don't diss your internal "check engine" light for coming on. We can re-calibrate it down the road. For now, be thankful for its warning.

OVER TIME: Cultivate a mindfulness practice. It will pay dividends big time.

Decode the Fear
A Brain That's TOO On The Ball

On a very basic level, the reason you feel anxiety related to public speaking is not emotional. It's chemical. You just have a brain that's especially dedicated to keeping you safe, in one specific arena, in the best way it can. That's what it evolved to do.

The human brain has evolved over thousands of years, but the oldest parts remain pretty much unchanged from caveman days. The chunk we're going to focus on here—quickly, and in easy-to-understand terms—is one of the oldest parts, called the mid-brain, or the limbic brain.

The mid-brain is brilliant at keeping us alive, and out of danger. It's what makes you turn the wheel on the car to avoid hitting a deer you don't consciously register until after your body has reacted. It's what alerts you to someone walking up behind you on a dark street.

It has other jobs, of course, but none more important than spotting a predator before it sees you.

And it has fiendishly smart tools to help us get out of harm's way, even when our rational mind tries to override the system and tell us, "Relax! You're just fine!"

The mid-brain spends a lot of time scanning the horizon in order to spot and avoid danger. Then it "wires in" the dangers it spots, so you'll instantly recognize the danger the next time you encounter it. Particularly efficient brains will alert you to danger the next time you encounter something that *might possibly lead* to a previous danger.

When the mid-brain is alerted to a predator or something else it identifies as a danger, it sends out neuro-chemicals in a flash. Those chemicals produce a set of physiological symptoms that we experience as nervousness or anxiety—or even panic, in extreme cases.

Check out some of my favorite books on the brain/body/spirit connection:

Daniel Goleman's *Emotional Intelligence*, Bantam Books, 1994

Candace Pert's *Molecules of Emotion*, Scribner, 1997

Daniel Gilbert's *Stumbling on Happiness*, Alfred Knopf, 2006.

Sharon Begley's *Train Your Mind, Change Your Brain*, Ballantine Books, 2007.

Norman Doidge's *The Brain That Changes Itself*, Silberman Books, 2007.

David Brooks, *The Social Animal*, Random House 2012

It's absolutely true that your brain wants to grab your attention—it wants you to know that there is some danger you should be alert to. But it's equally true that the physical symptoms you experience come from very specific demands on your body, designed to keep you safe in very specific ways.

Let's look at what it "feels" like to be nervous, and how your brain/body is attempting to help you.

Your heart starts pounding. This is often the first symptom of nervousness that people experience. It happens because your brain wants as much oxygen as possible to be directed to your heart, so you're ready to shoot that oxygenated blood out to your hands and feet, the better to punch or run your way out of danger. It's worked for tens of thousands of years; it still works today.

Your breathing changes, and it's hard to get a deep breath. The mid-brain makes your breath shallow so you won't noisily gulp air and give away your location to a nearby predator. Thousands of years ago, the predator was a tiger or bear. Today, it could be a masked robber or your boss. The brain will help you defend against both…whether you want it to, or not.

Your mouth gets dry, so you can't inhale and you choke yourself as you run for cover. Smart when you're hiding in the bushes; less useful when you're standing in the lobby waiting for an audition. Your brain doesn't know the difference. It just registers the danger as serious, maybe life-threatening.

Your vision changes. You may notice that it's hard to read, and all you see are blank faces staring at you. When your brain thinks you're in serious danger, it's interested in spotting two things. The first is a fast moving object headed your way—like a spear or boulder, or a tiger racing for you. The second is the eyes of the predator. Specifically, are those eyes zeroed in on you, or on someone else? In your mid-brain's lexicon, "Am I what's for dinner, or is the other guy?"

You can't hear as well because the mid-brain is less interested in the mid-range sounds of human speech. Instead, it's tuned to listen for signs that someone is sneaking up on you—the rustle of leaves, for example. And it's listening for the low growl of an animal, or the higher pitched whiz of a projectile missile. Is it listening for that middle range where people speak? Not so much.

Your stomach starts to do flips. The mid-brain pours out adrenalin into your bloodstream, so you have the extra power you need to do whatever you require. You have about twenty seconds worth of adrenalin, and it gets pumped out in one jolt. You feel the jolt of adrenalin, and then you live with the nausea that results from the chemical being in your stomach until it's metabolized through your system. That takes about ninety minutes.

You may have digestive distress because your blood is pulled away from your brain and most organs, so it can be mobilized by the heart, the hands, and the feet. It doesn't want to waste any energy on any body functions that aren't required for getting you to safety.

It's hard to think clearly because the blood has left the "smart" part of your brain, in the neocortex right behind your forehead. Indeed, the mid-brain doesn't want you to reason your way out of danger because it operates on the premise that instinctive reaction, without thought, will save your life. It does not want you pausing to think, "Hmmmm…Looks like that SUV is headed for me. Which way should I jump now? Or should I stay still and count on it to swerve?" That's a death-sentence thought pattern. Your mid-brain is happiest when it helps you react *now* and think *later*. This system was brilliant when we lived in the forest. It's less useful in the conference room or the concert hall.

You aren't crazy. When you have stage fright and think you can't hear, see, think, or breathe well, you're right!

That middle range where the human voice is heard *really is* squeezed out. The faces that look at you from the audience *really do* look like predators to your mid-brain. That brain fog you feel? *It's real.* The blood that was powering the smart front brain as you drove to work this morning is now in your heart, pumping blood out to the very feet that now are trying to make you walk off the stage, out of the auditorium, and back to your car—away from the "predators."

In short, it's how you're wired. In fact, anyone reading this comes from ancestors whose mid-brains did a good job of keeping their genetic pool alive over the centuries. So chances are good you have a highly effective mid-brain.

You can't "will" this away.

In fact, the more you try to ignore the symptoms of anxiety, the harder your body will work to make sure you know you are in danger: "Hi there! Listen. You should skip this meeting." Maybe it's a business meeting, maybe it's a sales call, or maybe it's a meeting to plan the PTA or church bake sale. It doesn't have to be high stakes; your brain doesn't always know the difference. The message comes with a sinking stomach and a little racing of the heart. But you know you have to show up, so you head for the conference room anyway. "Um, Hello?" That's your mid-brain trying to get your attention. Now your heart is beating faster. You need a glass of water as you see you're one of the last to arrive. Your hands may be sweating, and you may actually really need to sit down because of that rubbery feeling in your knees. "If you insist on staying here, you better not say a word. Got it?" The mid-brain is getting serious now.

But you have a question, something you really need to get answered. You can't think of another way to get the information, so you raise your hand.

Now your heart is truly pounding, and you can hear the blood in your ears, but not much else. "Hey, BUDDY! Get the heck OUT OF THE CONFERENCE ROOM! NOW!" The mid-brain is about to pull out all the stops to get you to leave the room and get out of danger. Let the other people stay and be eaten! That's not going to be your fate.

Yet, you stay anyway. And when you finally get called on, you stumble on your words, don't feel articulate, and aren't sure you even heard what the response was anyway. You can bet your mid-brain is going to make sure you mumble nothing more than, "Okay, thanks," as it robs you of the breath you need to support any additional sound.

You got the signals. You ignored them. They escalated. You ignored that. And your brain will remember for next time: "Bad things happen in the conference room." You better believe you'll be reminded before the next staff meeting—or whatever your equivalent experience might be...

Unless you break up the chain reaction.

When you stop fighting the anxiety reaction, and see what's behind it, you can start shifting the reason for the reaction...rather than trying to adjust the symptoms. We'll talk more about that later.

It's not worth having a meltdown or other emotional reaction to this chain reaction of anxiety. Not only are these feelings of fear not in your conscious control, but the fact that you're having them has nothing to do with your character, your integrity, your intelligence, your strength, or any other character trait you possess.

There's nothing wrong with you. Your body is doing exactly what it was designed to do. Recognize that this reaction, though unwanted, is an attempt by your brain/body to help you. Even that change in perspective can be enough to keep fear from escalating into panic. And for many readers, it will be enough to reduce the fear to a very manageable place.

Remember:

- You aren't crazy.
- Your brain is bathed in chemicals that, to varying degrees based on how hard your mid-brain is working to help you avoid danger, can change the way you see, hear, think, breathe, feel, and move.
- You can't "will" this away.
- It means nothing about you as a person.
- You CAN break up the chain reaction, or prevent it from happening in the first place.

Now it's time to learn a few methods so even when you are experiencing these symptoms, you can still perform well for your audience.

USE THESE IDEAS NOW!

Here are two powerful and simple ideas you can put to use right away to take advantage of what we know about the brain.

Breathe like a sleeping person.
As soon as you notice you're getting nervous, **consciously trick your mid-brain** by changing your breathing. In full fear mode, the mid-brain makes us breathe shallowly, and hold our breath on the inhale. To experience this shallow breathing, try this exercise now: Inhale shallowly on the count of 3, and hold your breath for 2 counts. Now exhale on the count of 3. Repeat 3 times, making sure not to stop between breaths. Now check into how you're feeling…which should be a bit anxious. Is your heart starting to pound?

Now, let's **reverse the pattern**. Inhale deeply on the count of 4, immediately exhale on the count of 4, and pause with nothing in your lungs for 2 counts. Repeat the inhale/exhale/pause pattern 3 more times. Notice that you feel calmer now. That's because this pattern mimics the breathing pattern of someone sleeping…and the mid-brain gets a signal that if the body is sleeping, it must be safe. As it relaxes, you start to feel things come back on line, and your hearing and sight improve. Your brain gets clearer. Your heart stops pounding. You can be more like "you" again!

I recommend that you practice these ideas—the calming breath and the flattened palm—before you need them. It will be easier to call on them whenever you are anxious, whether stage fright is the cause or not. Give your brain/body connection a minute to start to work.

Uncurl your fists.

A second way to trick your brain into relaxing has to do with calming the "fight" part of the fight, flight, or freeze response. Most people who find themselves in this reactive mode will notice that their fists ball up…the better to punch their way out of danger. Simply **open your hand and lay it flat somewhere.** That will start to send a signal that there's no longer a need to punch. Be careful about putting your hands on the arms of a chair; it's easy to grip the arms, and the brain will experience that in a way similar to a balled fist.

These exercises are purely mechanical ways to interrupt the flow of neuro-chemicals that produce the symptoms of nervousness. And there are other techniques to disentangle the energy of fear from the experience of performing. They're cutting-edge tools to help you change the things that parts of your brain think are dangerous. But my experience is that, for many people, these interventions will be enough to start shifting their attitudes toward—and for them to experience—stage fright.

Remember:

> **Breathe like a sleeping person.**

> **Open up your palm so it's not balled up in a fist, and send calming signals to your brain.**

Chapter Four

Meet Subby

The ancient mid-brain isn't just acting on its own. It's acting in reaction to beliefs and memories you have stored in your subconscious, which run like software behind the scenes.

It's a fascinating thing, that subconscious mind. I talk to mine all the time, and soon, maybe you will, too.

I call my subconscious mind "Subby" and I will here, too.

Here's one of the most fascinating things about our Subbys:

> **The subconscious mind believes everything you tell it, even the conflicting stuff.**

It believes, "I want to succeed." But it also believes, "I can't succeed more than my father/brother/sister has." So there's a quandary.

It believes, "I have a good idea I want to talk about." But it also believes, "I have to be perfect. I can't make a mistake." And you're stuck in fear, and silence.

The beliefs that get wired in there, in your subconscious mind, really have an impact.

"Children should be seen and not heard"—it's in there. You can guess how that impacts people who need to speak up in business meetings.

"Don't be boastful"—it's in there.

"Be careful! Don't make a mistake!" Imagine how many times you heard that, even before the age of seven! They're all in there.

"You gave a book report in second grade, but didn't finish the book, got caught, and got laughed at"—that's in there. Those beliefs, and who knows how many others, cause conflicting points of view.

One of the conflicting points of view has to win out, and it will always be the one that keeps you safest.

"I want to show them what our team's accomplished on this project," is never going to win over, "I could die of shame if I make a mistake," *unless* you clear up the conflict.

The great news is you don't need years of therapy or even a psychologist to work this stuff out.[1] There are some absolutely elegant, effective, cutting edge tools we use in our practice to help people work out those conflicts so the brain irons them out in private, instead of showing up RIGHT in the middle of a meeting.

Here's another interesting brain fact: Emotions run through the mid-brain. They run right through the amygdala—that walnut-sized part of your brain in charge of fight, flight, or freeze. Decisions to take any action also run through the mid-brain before you act. No human decides to take an action unless the action runs through that part of the brain.

From an evolutionary perspective, the amygdala offers a brilliant sorting device that goes something like this:

YOU: "I'm headed into those woods over there."
AMYGDALA: "Are you crazy? That's where the tiger came out at us last time! Don't you remember how awful that was? I bet you do because I'm pouring chemical into your body RIGHT NOW to make you sick about even considering going in those woods again. Sheesh!" (Quoth the amygdala, but at a speed faster than I can type a single letter).
YOU: "Okay. I'm headed toward the rocks instead."
AMYGDALA: "There are snakes over there, but at least you can hear those."
YOU: "Looks like it's the hammock for me."
AMYGDALA: "Good choice!"

---

1 That said, if you're being treated for anxiety or depression, or any other emotionally-based set of symptoms, I want to be completely clear that nothing I'm saying here is meant as a diagnosis, or as a suggestion to go off any prescription medication.

So the brain learns to tie certain circumstances to specific emotions.

Neuroscientists say that brain neurons that fire together, wire together. Let's say your mom made great mashed potatoes for Sunday dinner, and those were times of coziness and togetherness. Your brain tied "mashed potatoes" to "coziness and love," and now you're wired for potatoes as comfort food. In the face of a hard day, your brain casts around for what will soothe you and the answer is ready: mashed potatoes, stat!

Well, the same thing happens in terms of what the brain finds dangerous. Say you gave a book report in second grade, and it didn't go very well. Maybe you mispronounced a word. Maybe you just wore some out-of-fashion-with-seven-year-olds clothing.

People may have laughed. You may have experienced your face getting red and feeling hot, along with the classic brain freeze that happens when the blood leaves the neo-cortex, or the "smart" part of your brain. For some people, that's enough to wire in, "Giving book reports is dangerous." Other people may learn, "Standing in front of the class is dangerous." Others may learn, "Reading out loud is dangerous," as one former client discovered.

Armed with the information that book reports/all reports/reading anything you could have to report on is dangerous, the mid-brain will start to be vigilant for when those events might occur. When it spots an oral report on the horizon, it sends the chemicals out, and the chain reaction of fear starts to occur. "Avoid the book report! Danger ahead!"

Let's fast forward to today when you have to give a report to your colleagues at work, for example. If your mid-brain believes it's just book reports that are dangerous, you're probably not going to get very nervous. But if your mid-brain has wired in that you're in danger every time you give a report, it will send danger signals along the way, until you either finish the report, or do what the brain wants you to do: Avoid giving it.

Let's say you're one of the people who once had a bad experience standing in front of a group of people, reading or speaking. Maybe you once had a bad experience in front of an audience, and—whatever happened—you forgot a chunk of your talk, or you called the boss the wrong name, or you froze and forgot something important at the time—your subconscious mind may now want to protect you from the damaging feelings of shame or humiliation that washed over you then. It associates shame and humiliation with talking in front of live humans, so...BAM—it alerts you to danger: SHAME ahead! And it does what it can to keep you from talking.

Maybe you feel like you're an imposter, like you've risen too high, or aren't the "right" kind of person, or have the wrong hair color or weight on the scale, or whatever—your subconscious mind may want to protect you from being discovered and losing your reputation, or your friendships, or your self-esteem, or even your job. And it does what it can to keep you from exposing yourself: It tries to keep you from talking.

It's incredibly elegant, isn't it? Let's leave aside, for the moment, that it's not actually helpful. Let's leave aside that it's caused you some harm, and maybe a different kind of embarrassment or pain. Leave that aside.

Can you see the level at which this is really smart? The more you can appreciate that, the better off you'll be. This doesn't mean you have to live in such alarm forever. But appreciation for the elegance of the "solution" actually helps.

More Cool Brain Facts

A few other cool brain/body facts will help you understand what is happening, and why it doesn't work just to "pretend" the fear away.

Read this if you are interested; skip ahead to the next chapter if you want. This stuff isn't critical for you to understand. For some people, however, simply knowing some of these facts makes them relax, and see that there's nothing mysterious and out of control going on with them.

Your brain thinks in pictures, not words. Even in people who've never had sight from birth, the part of the brain responsible for vision lights up whether you're seeing something or imagining it.

Memory doesn't get stored away and then later pulled out whole, the way it went in. Brains will store away information in various parts of the brain that, for the sake of our shorthand, we'll just call files. When you meet someone for the first time, his or her name gets put in the short-term file. Sometimes, it doesn't make it into that file, and you can't recall the name even three minutes later. As the brain sorts through what to keep and what to let go, items of importance go into other files (or parts) of the brain.

That process is something scientists call "consolidation." That's the term for the way the brain converts short-term memory into mid- and long-term memory. In very simple terms, it distills the memory down to the most important data points, and it stores it away till you want it back. It might store one memory several different ways.

Your first kiss, maybe, gets associated under "kiss," under "boy" or "girl," under "fun things" or "daring things," under the time of year it happened, the way the light in the sunset looked, the smell of Head and Shoulders shampoo, etc.

When you want to get a memory out of the mid- or long-term memory file, your brain goes through something called, "reconsolidation." That is, it zips through the "files" to collect the various parts of the memory, and then it delivers the memory to the conscious mind to think or talk about.

Try this, right now. What was the best vacation you ever took? The memory that just popped up was probably easy to find, as it reconsolidated itself. That's because you've thought about it before, so the neural pathways were well traveled. Your brain had practice finding the right files to search through. Keep remembering it and notice how many more fragments of memory pop up.

Now try this: Remember the first time you drove a car on your own. Depending on your age, this memory may be easier or more difficult to recall…but it's likely taking some time, whatever your age. You don't commonly call for that memory (unless something spectacular happened that day), and it can take a while for enough bits to reconsolidate to give you a full picture of the day.

Here's why the idea of where memory goes in, and how it gets retrieved, matters: Part of the brain's job is to help you remember, as efficiently as possible, what things deliver pleasure and what things deliver danger. It doesn't have an easy time delivering dangerous things into the long-term memory files because it can take too long to get them back out. If it put "dark alley" in the long-term file, and it took as long to come up as your first day of driving has taken—you could be jumped and robbed and left for dead before you remember, "Oh, yeah. Don't go down those alone."

So when your brain grabs onto, "Putting yourself out for others to judge could make you want to die," that doesn't go into the long-term memory banks. It stays in the easier-to-access areas so it can be triggered easily…to keep you safe. If you need to be terrified to stay safe, that's cool with your brain.

The point is: Not all memory is equal. There is a reason your brain will keep rehashing the time you blanked on what to say or the time you couldn't answer a question on command. There is some evidence to suggest that when you can help the brain file that stuff in the long-term memory files, it doesn't get triggered…and you don't feel the fear the way you used to.

That's why understanding emotional neuroplasticity, sometimes called "energy psychology," is so helpful. Whether it's in the vein of EMDR (Eye Movement Desensitization and Reprogramming) or NLP (Neuro-Linguistic Programming) or EFT (Emotional Freedom Technique) or a variety of other cutting edge, brain-changing modalities, there's increasing evidence that people can change the way "memory" is stored and accessed, so as to take away the triggers to anxiety and fear.

Your subconscious doesn't do negatives. Most people have played the game, "Don't think of an elephant in the corner of the room." And, of course, the mind immediately pictures…the elephant in the corner of the room. That's because the brain has to form the picture of the elephant, and then a picture equal to "not that." Then it has to remind itself "Which 'not that' am I supposed to be avoiding, again?" At which point it delivers the image of an elephant in the corner of the room.

And the cycle goes on, as it bounces back and forth, essentially between "Not that" and "Not what? Not the elephant! Got it."

NOT thinking of something is not a resourceful way to approach the problem. The resourceful approach, that works with the way brains work, is to give the brain something else to picture. Then there's no room for the elephant. That's why, when we coach speakers, we never say, "Don't pace back and forth." We tell them, instead, "Plant yourself at this point in the talk."

When you know more about how the brain and the subconscious work together—and when you have some simple tools to "talk" to the brain in ways it understands, you may find that your anxiety is reduced to a manageable level. It's been our experience that many people find relief just by being armed with this knowledge. Some people need additional support, and that's where we're headed next.

Remember:

Subby believes everything you tell it—even the conflicting stuff.

One conflicting view will win out, and it will always be the one that Subby thinks keeps you safest.

TRY THIS NOW!

Start building a deliberate dialogue with Subby. You've already got the dialogue running ("You loser!" "You can't do that!" "You'll never be any good at this!"). We're just going to make it more deliberately positive and resourceful.

Here's a method of inquiry that's really effective for having a dialogue with Subby. It takes advantage of the way Subby wants to help and is actively working to help.

When you notice the first signs of anxiety starting up:

In that very moment, you might investigate yourself to determine what you're really afraid of. And the way to do it is to say to your Self something like this:

"Thanks for letting me know to be alert. I get the message." (And now notice that already you're probably starting to calm down some.)

"I'm grateful to you for protecting me now. The problem here is really about…" and then wait for something to pop into your head, or some area of your body to draw your attention. Don't ask it as a question. Open it as an area of curiosity without judgment. And take whatever you get, even if it seems whacky.

We had a client who tried this technique just today, and what he got was: "I'll die." On a rational level, that just seems nutty. But to his Subby, it wasn't nutty at all. It was a true potential. We helped Subby see that in this particular situation, death wasn't actually a likely or remotely possible outcome. And in a matter of minutes, his fear stepped back.

In fact, I just used this method of inquiry for myself, right now. As I was typing this, I noticed a little hitch in my stomach. I stopped, and said the words above, exactly as I typed them. And here's what I got:

"The problem here is really about…the readers might not believe that it's this simple to get good information from your subconscious mind, so they might stop reading and never get the help I have for them here."

Good to know. If I had blasted right by that, it would have come up somewhere else. Instead, I saw it, so I could have a talk with my subconscious mind that went something like this:

"Good to know. Thank you for alerting me to that danger. All parts of me are definitely aligned with wanting people to be able to dissolve their stage fright. And, the fact is that this line of inquiry really *is* this easy, most of the time. I choose to have confidence in my readers being at least as smart as I am, and that they'll experience this for themselves."

Problem solved for me.

Are all problems solved this easily? No. I wouldn't have such a thriving practice if they were. But some are. And it's a simple, elegant, and effective tool you can use anytime you want…even right in public…and no one but you and your Subby will be the wiser.

All anyone else will know is that once, you were silent. Now, you can speak.

And how cool will that be?

The Eight Buckets of Stage Fright

Everyone is different. Everyone's pain is unique. Everyone has a different story.

In our work with people with mild speaker anxiety, all the way to the seriously scared, we've identified eight buckets into which most people fall. Most people have one predominant bucket, with spill over into another. These buckets hold sets of beliefs or experiences that somehow clash with the circumstances of needing to speak in public. The greater the conflict, the more symptoms of stage fright the speaker endures.

See which bucket resonates most for you:

1. HAD A BAD EXPERIENCE.

You know who you are. You can tell me, in wretched detail, the minute-by-minute specifics of a presentation, or a moment in it, that went off the rails for you. It's not uncommon for me to hear that the audience probably didn't notice what went wrong. And it's not uncommon for me to hear that it will never be forgotten, or forgiven, by you.

This Bucket May Be A Good Place To Start If: You can describe a difficult performance experience—no matter how old you were, no matter how long ago it was.

What Might Help Right Now: You don't need to keep the memories fresh to do a better job next time, regardless of whether the bad experience happened out of the blue, or you can look back and take some lesson from it (prepare more thoroughly next time, or don't have three extra cups of coffee beforehand, for example).

Finally, take a page from aboriginal shamans, and "change" the past, on an energetic level. Imagine a timeline above your head that stretches out to the future and back to the past. It might go from left to right or right to left. It might go from behind you to in front of you.

Float above you, up in the timeline, starting where you are today. Go in the direction of the "past" and notice what you notice along the route back to the Bad Experience. There's nothing for you to do with what you notice except just notice it.

When you get to the Bad Experience, just imagine you can see it. Notice what you notice here. Then, go farther back to the moments *before* the Bad Experience, going to whatever was peaceful and calm, and maybe even fun and anticipatory, before the event. Notice that you don't feel what you felt in the Bad Experience. It feels okay now. Sweet, huh?

Now take that feeling up through the timeline and bring it to this present moment. Notice how things are subtly but elegantly shifted. Keep going, out into the future, taking the more empowered feeling forward in time. When you reach a point where you feel like, "Yep, that's as far as I need to go" simply intend that this more powerful feeling "stay" through the whole timeline, and come on back to now.

I'm no longer surprised how often people shift in huge ways when I lead them through this exercise.

One caveat: "Had a Bad Experience" people almost always fit in another bucket because something else set off the stage fright in the first place. But this bucket is the first one for you to clear.

2. IT NEEDS TO BE PERFECT/I NEED TO BE PERFECT.
One client in this group described herself as a "Type A on steroids." It's an apt description. The need for control is very intense in this group.

People with this type of stage fright use the specter of perfection to motivate themselves toward success. They tend to see limited choices about how they "have to" behave and appear in regular life, and in the realm of public speaking, they have an even smaller target for what "perfection" looks like. It's an especially tough version to have because so much of their wiring is tied into I Need To Be Perfect. They tend to beat themselves up for shortcomings, and they have a mean self-talk soundtrack running in the back of their minds: "You loser! How did you miss that?"

This Bucket Might Be A Good Place To Start If: You're someone who routinely over-delivers and still grades yourself with a "B." If you do the work or life equivalent of "extra credit work," this could be your bucket. If you demand of yourself brilliant material, exceeding what's practical, possible, and what's even required of the moment, start here. If you take great pains to present a perfect image, if how you look and come off matter to you more than to most mortals—if reading the phrase that compared you to "most mortals" gave you a twinge—start in this bucket.

What Might Help Right Now: Redefine what "perfect" looks like, at least in regards to what audiences want. Smooth gestures impress you, but they don't impress us as much. You don't get extra credit for delivering a flawless, safe, and boring talk. All you get is less of our attention next time you speak.

Most people don't see the world the way you do. We won't care about the run in your hose or the sentence you skipped if you make sure we leave your talk better than when we walked into the room. Launch your ideas at us; not your desired "perfection."

Audiences want to be in the presence of real people. You can't photoshop your life. People, in real life, say "um" and "you know." In real life, they spill coffee on themselves and get stuck in traffic. They forget what they were planning to say next and say something else instead. They wear white after Labor Day.

Not *you* of course. Except, sometimes, these things befall even you. If you keep letting that matter, and if you keep judging others to whom they happen, you won't see—and can never deliver—what actually matters most to audiences.

3. I CAN'T MAKE A MISTAKE.

Where the "Perfect" speakers are motivated to head toward success, the typical "I Can't Make A Mistake" people are motivated to avoid failure. It's a subtle but genuine distinction. These people sometimes hyper-focus on all the things that can go wrong, and they expect them to. They hold themselves to unreasonable standards: no ums or uhs. Smooth gestures, good jokes, perfectly spoken words, read or memorized flawlessly. But what they rehearse in their minds are all the mistakes they could make, and all the ways they'll be sabotaged by their inadequacies.

This Bucket Might Be A Good Place To Start If: You actively and obsessively imagine all the ways you could mess up: "I'll trip on the way up," "I'll forget what to say," "I'll go blank and they will sit there looking at me," "When they call on me, I won't be able to move out of my chair," or "I'll say 'um' and then I'll hear myself say it and I'll say it again…" Feeling like your job/credibility depends on a flawless performance (even if that is objectively true—which it rarely is) is another sign that you could have some baggage here. If you're very conscious about how you come off to others, and you are mean to yourself as you go through your day, you just found your bucket.

Finally, start here if you're someone who motivates yourself by beating yourself up about every mistake, no matter how small. My bet is you'll find out that you will always reach to do your best, even without being so self-punishing. And because you won't be visualizing so many missteps, you probably won't be materializing as many mistakes along the way.

What Might Help Right Now: Think of yourself as your own friend, and treat yourself accordingly. Be kinder to yourself. Trust yourself to handle whatever happens. Most of all, rehearse everything going *right*, not wrong. Trying to see all the disasters that could befall you so you are "ready" is not the best use of your limited time to prepare.

Don't rehearse for the problem. Put your energy and resources into rehearsing to be your solution.

At the same time, studies show it can be useful to review what you might do differently next time, and imagine yourself doing that. That way, you prime your brain to reach for more resourceful solutions in the future.

4. MESSAGES FROM CHILDHOOD.

These people really took to heart teachings we learned from parents, teachers, siblings, and the community at large. Those messages didn't get updated along the way. So it's like running the first generation of a word processing program on a new computer: Glitches are inevitable. Common messages include:

- Children should be seen and not heard.
- People in our family always/never…
- You have to be more successful than so-and-so, or you *can't* be more successful than so-and-so
- Don't be boastful and proud
- Ladies don't draw attention to themselves
- It's a sin to dance or act
- Never rest on your laurels
- You'll always have to work harder than anyone else, and settle for less
- People who look like me/act like me/come from my part of the world/from my economic background, etc., can attain only so much success
- You can't trust the boss (so I can't become the boss)

This Bucket Might Be A Good Place To Start If: If you got a ping in your stomach on any of the above beliefs, or suddenly remembered one of your own. If you can recall having heard adults around you, growing up, speak something similar, start here—even if you think it's had no impact. If you had anything that made you look or seem "different" from the *other kids* (speech impediment, major illness, extremes of wealth or poverty, parent with an odd career, etc.), start here.

What Might Help Right Now: Just like the operating systems on all your devices need some updating, so might you. Don't tell yourself you should just cut it out, and stop believing what the "younger you" once believed. Actively work with your subconscious to install new programming. Thank the younger you for keeping track of the lesson, and for working so hard to remember it and keep you out of harm's way. Then take a breath. Now tell your Subby, "It's now safe, at my current age, to let that go. In fact, [state whatever the updated belief could be]. You're free to have all the benefits of all of me at this age! Thank you for coming along and updating my programming… now."

5. I NEED TO SHOW A BETTER ME.

These people spend a lot of time, in all areas of their lives, trying to show how good they are at…whatever. These people heard lots of "not good enough" messages along the way, and they are determined not to be left in the "not good enough" pile. They tend to seek approval from others; they can't feel like they did a good job unless it's publicly acknowledged.

This Bucket Might Be A Good Place To Start If: You find yourself working hard to let others know that you're more than meets the eye. Others' impressions of you may be more important to you than your own. Are you starting to have a level of success that you fear you can't keep up with? Do you work your Ivy League degree or great reviews in at every chance? Have competitive vacations and hobbies? Other people may call you proud or insecure. You're just focused on the requirement to put your best foot forward, all the time—even if you need to shove it out there. If you hear yourself thinking, "I'll show them!" or "I'll prove them wrong" thoughts, especially related to performance, this is a good bucket for you to clear.

And if you hear yourself thinking, "I'm an imposter—they will find me out," this is your bucket for sure.

What Might Help Right Now: Try the exercises for "Perfect" and "Messages from Childhood."

In addition, try this. Get out a piece of paper and a pencil—not a pen. Draw a circle. Fill it with dots that stand in for all the ways you are "not good enough." You don't even have to have specific ways in mind. Just dot that baby up until Subby says, "That's it. Done."

Take a look at the circle. Notice how much more white space there is than dotted space? Even if your circle looks like the pocked surface of the moon, there is a whole lot more white space than dotted space. Ask your Subby to take it in. Ask your Subby to look for the open, white space on the page and in your life.

And be prepared to notice that you are subtly but genuinely happier and less hard on yourself. When you find yourself in a particularly stiff bout of "not good enough-ness," repeat the exercise. Over time, Subby will get it. And if there is some area of your life where you need to be a better you, go get the skills or perspective change or energetic shifts that will allow you actually to own the improvement. Otherwise, you'll always feel like an imposter and fear being caught.

6. DON'T BE A DISAPPOINTMENT.

There are two subsets here: Those who don't want to let themselves down, and those who are afraid of letting down someone else. One client I worked with had his grandfather as a constant, imaginary audience member. Granddad became a pharmacist at a time when it would have been tremendously difficult for someone of his background, and he raised his whole family up in status as a result. He also had died by the time our client was in grade school—but nonetheless, the client built his life so he would never be a disappointment to Granddad.

Both subsets here usually don't accept public acknowledgment of a good performance as good enough. Instead, they hold themselves to a seriously high inner standard. They use fear of failure as a motivator. While the "I *need* to be *perfect*" people are mean as snakes to themselves ("Pick up the pace, loser!" "You idiot!"), this group can tend to be kinder ("You can do this! You gotta come through here!"). The problem is, no accomplishment is ever enough. Just over the horizon, there is always a new way to let yourself down.

This Bucket Might Be A Good Place To Start If: You use fear of disaster as a means to motivate yourself. Being female, growing up poor, or being a minority makes it more likely that you have baggage here, purely because of the "prove yourself" messages that society at large sends. If you have a sense that you can never let down your guard, never relax, or you will get caught short, this would be a good bucket to clear.

What Might Help Right Now: If the person you fear disappointing is alive, consider having a conversation with him (or her). Tell the person exactly the lengths to which you're going to avoid disappointing him. Be specific about how this plays out in the realm of public speaking. Then let him respond. My bet is that you'll find out none of it actually matters.

Even if you can't actually have the conversation with the person, maybe because it's impractical, or too difficult, or because he isn't living now, imagine having it. Remember how your brain doesn't know the difference between imagination and reality? Let the person assure you, in your imagination, that the things that really matter—like love, for example—can never be jeopardized by anything you say or do in a business talk.

And if the person is *you*, if you're afraid of letting *you* down, have the conversation with an avatar of yourself. Just imagine a "you" sitting across from you. Tell that "you" what you're afraid of. Then switch places and respond to yourself. Don't try to talk "you" out of anything. Just have a reasonable discussion with yourself. Two keys: Literally switch places. Speak out loud and be open to whatever comes out of your mouth.

7. WHAT IF I'M ACTUALLY GOOD AT THIS?

This crowd has a tricky problem. The people in it want to succeed… but there's something about the price of success that scares them.

Sometimes, they have no idea what it is. Sometimes it might mean the possibility of being promoted, and having your friends at work now report to you—which jeopardizes your relationships. Sometimes it might mean attaining more success than the "anointed one" in your family of origin. I've had several clients who had the internal message that they couldn't exceed the success of their fathers. It wasn't that they weren't adequate to exceed Dad; it was that it would upset the whole family balance if they had greater success. Sometimes, the "reward" for being good at speaking is just more speaking. This bucket is a classic catch-22.

This Bucket Might Be A Good Place To Start If: You find yourself thinking, "I don't want to do any more presenting than I have to." Maybe your family has a delicate balance in which your success might seem to upset the apple cart. Maybe you fear losing your friends if you get promoted. Maybe you fear losing your job if you get promoted. You might also have a sense that "It's just not safe" to be in the spotlight, even if you don't know why.

What Might Help Right Now: If you know what the "consequences" are for being a stronger, more confident speaker, put them on a piece of paper. Take a good look at them.

Is being afraid of speaking the *only* way to avoid those consequences? And do you even need to avoid them at all? Maybe those beliefs have reached their sell-by date. If, for example, you can see that your colleagues who speak with more confidence than you do (so far!) aren't being boastful and showboaty, doesn't it stand to reason that you can be confident without getting yourself all puffed up?

You may suddenly see a window to a new way of being, and slip right through. Or you may need a few days, or weeks, to wrap your head around a new way of being in the world, with updated "software." Whatever it takes, it's worth going there, in our experience.

8. I DON'T REALLY KNOW WHAT I'M DOING/I'M NOT READY.

In this case, sometimes Subby is onto something real, and it's letting you know: "Hey, you aren't ready! You don't know the material well enough and you need to rehearse!" That's a message that you need to prepare better. At InVisible Light, we have a foolproof process for developing presentations that work for your audience, your business, and yourself, and simply using that process can eliminate this type of stage fright.

However, sometimes Subby believes you need to know way more than you actually need to know to do a good job for the audience. Subby is trapped back in the way the world is a mystery to very young kids, when they have no sense of how wide the gap is between what they know and what they don't know. If the gap seems huge, Subby is on the case to alert you to danger.

This Bucket Might Be A Good Place To Start If: You feel like you don't know how to prepare or deliver a presentation well, or you don't have a strong enough handle on your content. Sometimes people describe themselves as "being in over my head." You may feel that way only when you need to present, or only around *this* presentation, or you may feel that about life in general. Take note of which category you most fit because the way you'll deal with Subby will change as a result.

What Might Help Right Now: If you feel like you don't know enough about how to create and deliver a good presentation, get help to do it. We have a great guide that has a step-by-step process for creating the content for a business presentation that will work for your audience, your business, and yourself. It includes some great ideas for the performance of your material, so that your delivery is authentically bold.

We coach executives to create and deliver presentations that work in this age of Twitter.

But there are lots of coaches around, and many resources for creating and delivering content that transforms audiences. Do some research and discover which coach might resonate with you. A tip: If the coach talks about body language, that's an old-school, 1990s business school approach. Keep looking. We know so much more now, but you won't find it with that kind of coach.

If you feel like you don't have a good enough handle on your content, assess whether that's actually true. Most of the time, you'll discover that you are the expert in the room on your content. "I don't know the answer to your question, but I'll get back to you" is a perfectly valid response to a question you can't answer. If you accurately assess that you really don't know enough, you have some choices to make that will empower you to present with confidence: Get more information, narrow the scope of the presentation to what you *do* know, or find someone else to give it. "Becoming a nervous wreck about it" isn't a useful option.

If you feel like you don't know enough in general, do a realistic assessment of whether that's true. Are you expert *enough* to deliver your material? That's all most audiences need.

Maybe you need to acquire more information, and Subby has it right. In that case, go get it. Metabolize the material and then share it with us.

But if you chronically feel like "I don't know enough to do a good job," and you've got a solid process to develop and deliver your talk, *and* you are in command of the material enough to deliver it, take a look at Bucket #5: I Need To Show A Better Me. Chances are, you have some work to do there.

What bucket resonates most for you?

Can you see yourself in more than one of them? Do the exercises I've listed and you may discover your speaker anxiety lifting to a point where it feels more manageable.

And "more manageable" makes a big difference. It makes the entire difference for some people, by moving them from, "I hate this and will do anything to avoid speaking," to "It's actually worth it to be able to speak up for my position/cause/perspective."

You don't have to be totally free from fear to manage it well enough to take command of your voice and use it effectively. More of you will be in this category than any other.

Some of you will have a more complicated string of reactions to untie. In the next chapter, we'll look at some stories of people who experienced complicated stage fright—including me.

Chapter
Six

Complicated State Fright

When I had stage fright for all that time I mentioned at the opening of this book, I was squarely in the "What if I'm actually good at this?" bucket. The family I was born into—as well as my perfectly great "practice husband"—didn't like my choice to act. For various reasons, it was too threatening to them.

But the run of my play kept getting extended, and the evidence was mounting that I was pretty good at something they disliked. My Subby went into paroxysms over how to keep me safe in their love and still keep acting. Fearing theatre was the best solution my Subby could find, and it did a spectacular job of keeping me safe in my family.

It even helped me by not letting me miss being in theatre when I watched others act because I couldn't be in a theatre even as an audience member at the magic "five minute mark"—the point at which the stage manager tells the actors there are five minutes till curtain.

It was a conflict I didn't see until I understood the secret that stage fright happens as the solution to a higher order problem.

I work with people to help deconstruct their conflicting beliefs and love doing it. Sometimes speakers have stuff going on in more than one bucket. And, in cases of severe speaker anxiety, sometimes people even have come to fear being afraid.

Some brains get caught in a loop of alarm, and the people with those brains are said to have PTSD, or post-traumatic stress disorder. It's what results from the mid-brain being unable to stand down and turn off.

While science is still looking for the reasons why some brains get stuck in a constant loop of learned "danger" signals, there's no doubt that people with PTSD react to otherwise benign stimuli as if they were life-threatening.

The same thing is true of people with severe stage fright and performance anxiety. In fact, anyone with a phobia is wired to fear an object or experience, and then become wired to fear the fear. Over time, some people see the fear spread to previously "safe" objects or experiences.

At InVisible Light, we once worked with a marketing VP whom we'll call Carol here. Carol was used to giving presentations that included slides. She had a strong preference for standing next to her computer and pressing the "enter" key to advance the slide. She felt stuck next to the computer, and she said she wanted to walk around. We tried to get her to take a wireless remote slide advancer. Carol refused.

That made no sense to us. It didn't seem to make sense to Carol either, who was still complaining about being stuck next to her laptop, but refusing to adopt the solution to her stuckness.

So I pressed her: "Use the remote!" Her team members in the workshop with her pressured her as well, until there was no longer any way around it. Suddenly, she blurted out that it "terrified" her, and she didn't see how she could give the presentation at all. She broke out in a sweat and had to sit down.

We took a break, and I sat with her to talk about the situation. A little quiet digging around turned up a surprising brain-fear intersection: She had broken her grandfather's TV remote as a child and been punished so severely that she wasn't about to use a remote *anything*, ever again. Until that moment, she hadn't put two and two together because she kept finding ways to avoid the feared object.

Carol wasn't nuts. Her brain had wired together "remote control" with "spanked and humiliated," and her system wasn't about to let her walk into that danger again—especially not in front of her colleagues. We used a simple method to decouple the ideas, and within twenty minutes, she was up and joking around, remote in hand.

If Carol hadn't gotten the tools to change the way her brain reacted to the remote slide advancer, she may or may not have progressed to no longer being fearful not just of the remote, but any situation in which she might be required to use one. She certainly had been on her way until she said she couldn't give the presentation at all.

Your Subby is working to help you. You may not like the kind of help it's offering. But it changes everything if you understand that it *is* helping, and *how* it's helping.

Let's take Jose, a self-avowed perfectionist. He feels most in control and confident when he feels in command of the details. He's clear that his fear is about making a mistake, which to him can look like a lot of things. Here is part of his actual list of possible mistakes:

- saying "um" or "uh"
- pausing too long before answering a question
- giving the wrong answer to a question
- having a typo in his slides
- having shaky hands when he needs to take a sip of water
- needing to take a sip of water
- mispronouncing something
- speaking too quickly
- speaking too slowly
- not being entertaining
- not being serious enough
- being dull
- forgetting what he's saying
- making a mistake that he doesn't hear himself make and doesn't correct
- hearing himself make a mistake
- forgetting someone's name
- etc. etc. etc.

There's room for error in virtually everything Jose could do. So his brain helped him prevent mistakes by making him freeze. If he can't talk, he can't make a mistake. Brilliant solution! Except...bad for Jose's career trajectory.

While there are things on this list that Jose can control—typos on his slides, for example—there are many others he can't. His brain saw the emotional equivalent of quick sand at every turn. So it did what it could to keep him safe by not letting him speak.

We helped Jose upgrade his view of what perfect was, at least in regard to giving presentations. It unlocked him, and he became such a good advocate for his projects that he received three promotions in an eighteen-month period.

Gail is another example. Gail is the daughter of a preacher, raised in a family where "people like us always" did things a certain way, and "never" did certain other things. One of the things people like her "never" did was call attention to themselves.

Gail's subconscious was completely down with helping her do just that. Since Gail's job required her to speak to her team periodically, her Subby had its work cut out for it. Subby sent signals that literally caused her to speak so quietly that she was hard to hear. She couldn't make eye contact with her audience.

If Gail accidently connected with someone, she experienced a jolt of what she described as energetic electricity through her body that felt like she was being electrocuted. Her brain wanted her to sit down and stop being bold. It didn't care what her job description said. The rules are clear: People like us never call attention to ourselves, period.

For Gail, the trick was to help Subby see the hyper quiet as *worse* than shouting and being heard. It was a two-minute fix, and it's lasted for years.

Brianne is another great example of someone whose stage fright symptoms are actually signals meant to protect her. Brianne never liked being in the spotlight, so she never was in the school play, on the pompom squad, or on the debate team. That was a sad but smart choice, for her. But then her daughters went to school, and she began to have opinions about how the school was being run. She had the choice to speak up, or to ignore what she didn't like.

Ignoring the problems worked only so long. Then the school system proposed a significant change in the way gifted and talented kids were treated, and her two girls were in jeopardy of being shoved out of a program in which they'd been thriving. Brianne started attending PTA meetings, and she found herself with a queasy stomach each time she heard herself even think a question. Her first step was to try to talk others into asking her questions for her. But her recruits found her questions so potent that they wanted her to take credit for them. In short order, they were pushing her to the mic, or speaking her suggestions, and then pointing her out.

No longer in charge of her destiny, Brianne started to feel nausea when she entered the school. Her brain understood what the deal was: She could be pointed at and asked for more information at the whim of someone else, or she could stay home. Better to prevent herself from walking in the building in the first place!

When Brianne could reframe the situation to see that she wasn't hogging attention for herself or her daughters, but shining a light on a situation that no one else could change but her, the anxiety symptoms released their grip enough that she could become an effective, efficient advocate. She never got to the point of being supremely comfortable. But she no longer had to pass scribbled talking points to others to speak on her behalf.

Each of these people got real help from my company to change the situation. They came to understand how their brains were "helping," and we found ways to recruit their hyper-alert systems to help in a more resourceful way.

You can work with your brain/body to calm it down before, during, and after an attack of performance anxiety.

In the next chapter, we'll share some of the cool techniques for dismantling complicated stage fright that we used with the clients above, and many others.

Dissolve The Triggers

There's a relatively new field, called energy psychology (EP), that offers a variety of ways essentially to rewire the way your brain and body process trauma and stressors like speaking in public. They are next generation techniques for breaking up fear and fear-based reactions.

Many of these techniques are based on traditional acupuncture/acupressure teachings. Because the field is so new, there are few classical double-blind studies to demonstrate how effective this work is. More are being done every year.

I use a variety of techniques to help our clients, and I love the results I've witnessed. There are many things to love about EP in general, and they seem to apply across the board.

First, you don't have to believe it will work in order for it to work. Skeptics get the same results as people who readily embrace non-traditional health coaching.

It's easy to learn to use some of these techniques on your own. You don't have to become an expert in them to get good results for yourself. And while you may move faster with a professional practitioner, you can get surprisingly good results with some focused work on yourself, by yourself.

These techniques generally work quickly—sometimes an issue will clear in a single session. More often, it can take a few sessions. But what about the 2 ½ *years* it took for me to be able to walk into a theatre, after I started experiencing stage fright? If I'd had these tools then, my bet is it would have taken more like 2 ½ weeks. Or less.

The results seem to stand up over time. Once you've shifted something, it stays shifted. There may be another aspect of the situation that pops up. I think of this process as being like peeling layers of an onion. Once you remove the top layer, it doesn't jump back on the onion. Same here.

I especially like EP for stage fright and performance anxiety because you don't have to re-experience your stage fright in order to work with it; you just have to know that you have it, and that you want to shift it.

So you don't have to re-traumatize your brain in this work. Since the brain doesn't know the difference between actually experiencing something and imagining it, that is a big deal.

You can use EP prior to a situation that could provoke possible stage fright to prevent the problem from *that* performance.

There's one technique you can use when you are in the midst of stage fright, without anyone knowing you're doing so.

And sometimes this technique has great by-products. It can clear up traumas you didn't even know you had. It's common for people to come to me to work on speaker anxiety, for example, and suddenly see an improvement in their golf games. Because a person has spill-over effect from one issue into another, you can end up clearing a lot more than you bargained for.

Does it sound too good to be true? That's partly why it took me so long to check it out once I learned about EP. I didn't believe it either! In fact, I believed that you had to work hard, that you had to experience angst and turmoil in order to make progress, and that dissolving the fear had to take a long time.

I was wrong on all counts.

Here are a few things you need to know about EP before we go further.

1. In EP, the person with the issues is the one doing the work. If you use the techniques we'll describe here, know that *you* are making the shifts in yourself. No one else can do it for you, even if someone else is guiding your session.
2. While this work seeks to be painless—and almost always is— know that you can end up stirring up some deep trauma or memories you didn't even realize you had. You need to be pre-pared for that before you begin, in case you are one of the rare people for whom this happens.
3. The shifts you can accomplish with this work can be subtle, or they can be profound. But they are real. That is why it's not considered ethical, for example, for a practitioner to work with a client who is involved in a lawsuit. Because it is so easy to shift trauma out of a person's psyche and energy field, the client can

end up being a poor witness in his own behalf. It can be hard for a jury to buy that the person has been emotionally damaged by an accident, for example, if he appears to be as dispassionate as one might be once he has used EP to clear the trauma.

4. It is a relatively young field. And while I am not personally aware of adverse reactions to the work, that doesn't mean that they can't occur.

After you read more about some of these techniques, you can decide whether or not to use them to try to clear your performance anxiety.

There are literally dozens of techniques one could use to clear performance anxiety. I work with many, but two in particular. We use them with clients in person and on the phone.

You can often find expert practitioners in your local area to help you use these modalities. It's easy to get materials for you to learn to use them on your own. I urge you to find out more about these particular techniques:

TAT®, or Tapas Acupressure Technique. This technique is great for clearing trauma in particular. Tapas Fleming created it out of her work as an acupuncturist. She was looking for faster and deeper ways to work with her clients than she could with traditional Chinese medicine. She has created a truly great technique, which has changed my life (and the lives of many of my clients) profoundly. It works with focused attention directed on a set of specific phrases, while you hold a specific set of acupressure points on your head. Each round of work takes about 10-20 minutes to accomplish. It's easy enough for a child to do on his or her own.

There is a great study about the impact of TAT", conducted by NIH and Kaiser Permanente in Portland, Oregon. That study took subjects with a pretty intractable issue of weight loss and maintenance and looked at what kinds of approaches might work. TAT" was the only one that resulted in people taking off significant weight, and keeping it off.

Tapas's work changed my life. My brother used to go off the grid for months at a time, but in this instance, he had been silent for eighteen months. No one had heard from or seen him, as far as we knew. In the Denver airport, on my way to a meeting, I learned from the police that my brother's body had been found in the woods in Virginia Beach. It just so happened that Tapas was teaching a workshop at this meeting, and it happened that I attended. In twenty minutes of working with Tapas, I went from numb to accepting, angry to forgiving.

Twenty minutes. In fact, the event was recorded on audio tape and is accessible through Tapas's website, www.TATLife.com. I invite you to hear the transformation for yourself. Tapas's tagline is "Real Change. Real Easy." From what I have experienced, it's true.

I use TAT® with many clients with speaker anxiety, and I use it often. I love that it's gentle, it's deep, and it transforms lives.

Be Set Free Fast®, or BSFF® is the work of Dr. Larry Nims, a psychologist who lives in Phoenix, Arizona.

BSFF® works directly with the subconscious essentially to rewire the way you connect to old issues, beliefs, memories, experiences, traumas, and other problems. It works through a set of instructions, delivered in a specific way to the subconscious, and is tied to a cue word. From that time on, you can say or think the cue word to trigger the entire set of instructions and eliminate the problem back to its roots.

BSFF® is particularly useful for executives, which is why I use it so often. There are no physical steps involved, so it's invisible to on-lookers. Because it can be done silently, without drawing attention to you, it's easy to use in public—such as in the middle of a meeting, an audition, or actual performance. You can learn more about this great technique by going to www.besetfreefast.com.

Many theories exist about how and why BSFF® works, though no one knows for sure. What I've observed, from my personal experience, and from using it with many people, is that it's doing *something* to help people shed unhelpful behaviors, emotions, thoughts, memories, and sensations. And it happens with surprising grace and ease.

There are two other techniques I use occasionally. The first is EFT, sometimes called "tapping." It was created by Dr. Gary Craig, who saw such potential in it that he made the teachings widely available so many people could learn, use, and benefit from it. It was the first EP technique I learned, and I still use it when people ask for it directly. If you're looking for an energy-based practitioner, you'll probably find an EFT practitioner very near you.

EFT works by tuning into the issue and tapping on specific acupressure points, while speaking various statements. It's an easy sequence to learn, and it doesn't take too long to do. Most of the clinical research into the effectiveness of EP is centered around EFT.

The second is an absolutely elegant and effective technique called Ask and Receive, created by Sandi Radomski and Tom Atschuler. Ask and Receive is believed to work from the point of pure potential, wherein you access the deepest wisdom of your body/mind/spirit and make profound shifts, following five simple statements. I love this method, and I'm using it with clients with increasing frequency.

If you'd like to know more about the entire body of work called "Energy Psychology," check out the Association for Comprehensive Energy Psychology at www.energypsych.org.

A variety of truly transformational, awesome techniques are out there that can help you shift the underlying thoughts, memories, emotions, beliefs, sensations, issues, and problems that may be "helping" you in ways that are less than helpful. Whether you use the techniques I've named here, or others, know that they're worth exploring if your nerves and anxiety aren't shifting as quickly or deeply as you'd like.

Chapter Eight

Deliver Your Voice

As I considered what stories of transformation to share with you, these five clients popped up almost immediately.

These clients were brave to embrace the help and the opportunity for transformation. At InVisible Light, we used a variety of tools to help them, but all used at least some BSFF® and TAT®.

As with all the stories in this book, I've changed the names of the people whose stories you'll read. In our work, we promise clients anonymity, and we're holding to it here.

Our goal is to help clients to speak with authority, authenticity, confidence, and verve—and to outgrow the need for us. We train, guide, and support them—but the credit for what they accomplish goes 100 percent to them.

Each one of them did the work that resulted in being able to speak their ideas in an authentic, compelling way. They found the freedom to deliver their voices to the discussion, and the courage to speak and lead.

Carol Ann came to me from the alternative health care world where she was a practitioner. She had to deliver a speech that would determine the fate of a project dear to her heart. It was up to Carol Ann to make the case for why her project should be funded and carried out.

And she was nervous. "Really, really nervous. Really nervous. Just short of panic. Just really, really nervous." In Carol Ann, "nervous" was experienced as a sick stomach, heart palpitations simply thinking about the event, and feeling like she had "scrambled eggs instead of brains." Her fear was so great that it was a 10 on a scale of 0 to 10, with 0 being "This is no problem at all" and 10 being "This is so bad we should call 911."

This scale is commonly called a SUDS scale, for "Subjective Units of Distress." We use it because the brain, you will recall, tends to believe that what it feels now is what it will always feel.

Carol Ann was at a 10 when she thought about the speech, and at a 10 when she thought about having to answer follow-up questions. She was a 5 when she thought about preparing for the speech. So we went to work on clearing what we could about the speech.

I tuned into what she was saying, she used her cue word, and by the end of the hour, she described herself as a 0 on the scale when she thought about giving the speech. The first order problem that her stage fright was serving was to keep her from feeling personally judged and found wanting. She was able to see the project, much as she loved it, as separate from herself. She aligned with the fact that approval or rejection of the project would impact the way she spent her time, and how excited she would be to come to work. But it would mean nothing about her as a person, either way.

Just before our time was up, I tested her. "Stand up and start giving me the speech now." Carol Ann stood right up and gathered her forces to start talking, even though she had no idea I would ask her to do so. Still, she was a zero on the SUDS scale. She was thrilled.

Five days later, she gave her speech. I spoke with her afterwards. "How was it?" I asked, expecting to hear good news.

"Awful!" she replied. "I was very nervous beforehand. The minute I woke up that day, I was a wreck!"

I was shocked. "Was the whole thing awful?" I asked, worried that somehow this time, BSFF® didn't work.

"Oh, it was fine as soon as I stood up. In fact, it was so fine, that it was confusing. I got through the speech great. I answered all the questions, even the ones that were hardballs, and I really nailed my close. It was even fun to do. Then I sat down and got nervous again. It was terrible."

All I could do was laugh. Carol Ann's experience reminded me about another important aspect of the "brain has no imagination" rule: the subconscious works literally. We had worked to clear every minute of the speech, from the moment she stood up to walk to the front of the room, to the moment she sat down. And it did work for THAT! But we hadn't cleared any of the fear related to the before and after of the presentation. The subconscious truly worked on a literal basis.

Now I always focus a portion of my private client coaching work on the "before and after presentation" period, all due to what Carol Ann and I learned together. And so should you, for yourself.

Meanwhile, Carol has been able to speak with such confidence in the community that she's been able to grow her practice from part-time to full-time.

Dan was a former college football player and a completely charming guy. His job rarely required him to speak to a group of people. But when it did, he found it impossible to do so without beta blockers. Beta blockers are a drug that makes the heart beat in a slower, calm rhythm. It's commonly prescribed for people who experience heart rhythm problems, or arrhythmia. It's also found an off-label use for anxious speakers. Since the feel of a racing heart puts some speakers into full stage fright, beta blockers make sense, because the racing never starts.

Dan's problem was that his office was short-staffed, and he found he was being called on to speak without warning. He wanted something more reliable than pills, he said, since he might not be able to take them in time.

So we played around. We cleared all kinds of things Dan could tell me he thought while he was speaking: "I can't do this without the pill. They can see the heart pounding out of my chest. My dad died of a heart attack, so these impromptu talks really could kill me." Because, in Dan's case, his stage fright was the solution for the real problem: "I'm afraid of feeling a rapidly beating heart because it makes me fear I'll die like my dad did."

We cleared, "I'm afraid of a racing heart," and everything related to that we could find. We cleared stuff for forty-five minutes, one thing after the other.

Now comes the time in the session to test the results. "Okay, Dan. Imagine you are asked to run the meeting for your boss…" I couldn't even finish the scenario before he grabbed his chest and said, "Oh my God. There it goes. It's starting!"

I thought fast and remembered the lessons Carol Ann cemented for me: The subconscious is literal; the brain has no imagination.

Then I told Dan, "Use the cue word to ask your heart to stop pounding, right now."

Dan used his cue word. And before I could think of what to do next—should we attack the situation this way or that way?—I saw the most curious look flash across Dan's face.

"Oh. My. God." He was stammering. "It worked. I asked it to stop pounding and it did. On a dime."

We were both looking at each other, amazed. From then on, Dan used his cue instead of his pill (though I want to be on record right now as saying we didn't then and don't now ever tell people to go off their medication, no matter what the medication might be).

I will forever remember the lesson Dan cemented for me: Try the easiest path first. It just might work.

Meanwhile, Dan now can speak up in meetings without fearing his own fear response. He's been promoted two times since we started work together, and he is now running the entire sales organization at a very large company. You almost certainly have that company's products in your home today.

Meredith came to work with us feeling fairly confident as a presenter. As an identified high-potential employee, she was starting to attract attention around her enormous, multi-national corporation. She was invited to speak about her team's recent success in front of an audience of the 400 most significant leaders in the company.

We were engaged to help Meredith prepare the message and performance she would deliver. Meredith worked brilliantly and diligently to prepare her talk. She embraced the things we teach that actually make speakers effective in front of an audience, and she was able to let go of outdated conventional wisdom about how speakers "should be" on stage. She rehearsed thoroughly. She was ready to be authentic and bold. She did everything right.

Then she got nervous.

She easily recognized that as a "serial over-preparer," as she called herself, there was nothing else she could do to deliver brilliantly than just to show up and trust her preparation was watertight. What jump-started her nerves was the higher order problem of not being able to control every aspect of the presentation.

But because she was brave and committed to doing the best job she could, she decided not to ignore the nerves, or pretend they weren't there. She came for more help.

Inside of thirty minutes, Meredith was able to learn and deploy the breathing and mindfulness exercises I discussed earlier in this book, and she noticed a real reduction in her anxiety levels. We next used BSFF® to shift out some unhelpful thoughts about specific people who would be in the room.

When she presented, Meredith rocked the joint. In fact, she was noticed by a very senior leader in the business and promoted within months of the presentation—leapfrogging several levels.

Meredith's story is one that many people wish for themselves. Again, we don't take credit for the incredible and deserved returns to her investment of time, resources, and Self. But Meredith was *ready to be ready* to deliver, so she reached out for help.

The truth is that speakers can be nervous *and* still do a terrific job of connecting to the audience, and having that audience carry their message out of the meeting.

Meredith would have done a fine job, without the extra help. But because she was willing to challenge herself to remove as many barriers as possible between herself and the audience, she ended up with a result that not even she would have predicted.

So many clients we've worked with have stepped up for themselves and stopped trying to gut their anxiety out alone. It's always an honor to help them, and to hear about what they're able to make happen in their careers and personal lives as a result. But few stories make me as proud as I am of **Rhiann.**

Rhiann worked for a small bio-tech company for over a decade. If people wanted something done, they went to Rhiann. She had an official title in the marketing department, but people used her as a "fixer" for all sorts of problems, from personnel issues to PR to Board strategy. People sought her out to be on their teams. From what I observed, Rhiann was doing the work of several people. She hadn't been promoted in years.

We were brought in to coach senior executives in a lengthy presentation, and there was a component of the message that rightly belonged to her to speak. It was her team, her work, and her success. But everyone in the room assumed someone else would speak it. As they debated just who that would be, and as I kept asking why it wouldn't be Rhiann speaking for herself, I learned that Rhiann never addressed audiences in formal settings. She only would speak to small, fairly informal meetings. She herself verified that it was true: "I HATE presenting and I won't do it."

With the backing of the CEO, we got Rhiann to agree to let us coach her to present this teeny portion of the meeting. If she ended up being too nervous, we told her she could back out and have it delivered by someone else.

I was taking a page right out of my own history. When I was too afraid to act, my director told me I could quit at any time, just to give the role a try. I did, and it made all the difference to me in my career and personal life. Sometimes, just letting yourself off the hook, knowing there's an "out," relieves enough pressure to let a scared speaker (or actor) say "Yes" to him- or herself.

It was rocky for Rhiann. She had almost no fun at all preparing her message. She had almost no fun rehearsing. She had almost no fun delivering her message. That's one way to look at the picture.

Here's another lens, though. Rhiann didn't experience the hives and nausea she normally would have lived through. She saw a pattern in her desire to stand in the shadow, safely helping people and getting no credit herself. She started to let go of the belief that the company should just notice and decide to promote her if she delivered marvelously on everything everyone asked of her. She saw her stage fright for what it was: the solution to the bigger problem of feeling like she couldn't ask for what she wanted without being "too big for her britches."

Here's a third lens: This company is small enough that people knew that "Rhiann doesn't present." But there she was, standing in the literal spotlight, sharing her ideas. People heard those ideas *out of her mouth*. Her colleagues were proud of her, and not nervous for her—because they didn't see her nerves.

Rhiann didn't eliminate all the anxiety by the time she presented, but she eliminated enough to be able to deliver *that* talk. And she kept working, so today she is able to speak with freedom in front of any audience.

Finally, here's another lens: Rhiann has been promoted multiple levels since we first met and worked with her. The most exhilarating presentation she's given to date?

The one in which she made the case for her first promotion. It worked.

The last story I want to tell is about **Ahmed**. Ahmed was someone who rocketed through his company, moving with record speed even through the ranks of an identified "hi po" (high potential) program. These programs are launched in companies to identify up-and-comers, with the intention of moving future leaders into and through a wide variety of business units and disciplines. This way, they're exposed to and familiar with what's going on across the enterprise.

These people are not just smart. They've been the smartest people in the room most of their lives. They have a level of confidence that envelops them, and that most others around them describe in almost visceral terms: "You feel him come into the room before you see him" or "You just feel good to be in her presence."

In other words, you don't land in one of these programs if you are someone with obvious speaker anxiety. And having speaker anxiety is certainly not in such a person's self-definition.

So Ahmed was surprised to learn that, despite his dual JD and MBA from an Ivy League school, despite the fact that he could hold forth on most topics with just about anybody, he was rendered almost speechless when he was called on to talk about company matters outside his company.

It's pretty common that we see clients who are "fine if I know the audience" or even "fine if I don't know the audience." That people can have enough confidence to speak in front of a particular audience but not another is a phenomenon with which we're very familiar.

But it was news to Ahmed. It challenged his view of himself to the point where he was rattling his mentor. And it was his mentor who sought our help, not Ahmed.

Ahmed was angry about being put with us. Again, pretty common. I know I'm in a foul mood when I go to get my teeth cleaned because they'll nail me for not flossing as much as I'm supposed to, and I'll leave there feeling bad about myself. Ahmed was already feeling bad about himself, and he felt that talking about what was going on would only make him feel worse.

Fortunately, it didn't take long for Ahmed to let down his guard. Almost immediately, we predicted what we believed to be the source of the problem. (It was the "Messages From Childhood" bucket, about who his family could safely share information with and who was dangerous to them.) We knocked it out pretty quickly.

Ahmed even sought the opportunity to speak to outsiders to test the results of our work. That's how, ten days after our last session, I came to have a video upload of Ahmed delivering a ten minute TED-Talk presentation on a specific tool he created to collapse barriers to innovative thinking.

He did a great job.

Along with the upload of the talk came this message:

> I would have stunted my own growth, and the growth I can facilitate in others, if I had stayed comfortable with my fear.... [F]rom you, I learned the power of acknowledging it, rather than denying it....I'm taking forward the tools you taught me, and the confidence I now own no matter who the audience might be. The possibilities are endless for what I can inspire in others, as a result of taking...your dare.

We agree. And we want it for you, too.

TRY THIS NOW!

You're ready for the second big secret no one tells you about stage fright:

You can be anxious and still do a good job.

The goal of this book, and my coaching, is to help you face a crowd with confidence.

But you don't have to go through a single exercise or implement a single idea to get more freedom as long as you keep this fact in mind: You can deliver a great presentation and *still* experience anxiety.

That's the truth. Being anxious doesn't doom you to failure, just like being confident doesn't guarantee success. In fact, some of the most confident speakers we've seen are full of hot air and empty calorie messages.

Absolutely, I want you to experience more anticipation and less anxiety. I hope you're able to be conscious and present with your audience, rather than having an out-of-body experience. We expect that you will, one day, actually look forward to delivering presentations of all kinds, to all kinds of audiences.

Between here and there, between now and getting those results, you need to know that being anxious isn't going to harm you. Anxiety doesn't need to stop you from delivering a smart message that resonates with and transforms your listeners.

But your fear of being anxious *could* stop you. It's your job not to let it.

By now, you know that the anxiety you experience is a cascade of chemicals, triggered by the mind/body/spirit as a way of helping you defend against something it fears will happen if/when you speak.

Sometimes people get anxious about being anxious. They so dread the stomach churning, heart pounding that visits them before they speak that they start to feel anxious about getting anxious. That starts the chemical cocktail hour rolling, and you're off to the races. Or the bathroom, as the case may be.

Here's the thing, though. If you let yourself stay stuck in the place of fearing fear, you'll never give yourself the opportunity to get out there and be better than you were before. And people won't get the gift of being able to hear you advocate for your ideas and programs, so they can take advantage of what you know and can help them do after the presentation ends.

You were scared when you learned to ride a bicycle, but you wanted freedom badly enough that you rode anyway. You were afraid when you learned to swim, but you wanted freedom badly enough that you swam anyway.

Remember when you first learned to drive, or asked someone on a date, or tried a new baseball pitch out, or jumped a level in school, or tackled a multi-page recipe—all kinds of things that were new to you and inspired fear, but which felt worth doing enough that you pushed through the fear and got to the other side. Remember those things?

Believe me when I tell you that public speaking is just as important. That the results on the other end are just as rewarding as evidenced by the success of the people whose stories I just shared—people who felt anxiety, yet still were able to do well in front of an audience. In the same way, the freedom you'll have, when you conquer the anxiety and come out the other side, and the power you'll have when you get on the other side—all of that is WORTH IT. It's worth standing up to the anxiety and doing it anyway.

Don't wait to become fearless. Become fearless by going out there, using what you know, and seeing the results from the audience members' point of view. They won't care if you're nervous, and they probably won't even notice you're nervous, if you make them feel better or wiser or more knowledgeable than they were before you began your presentation.

And you can do that…but only if you don't back down. Only if you remember that you can feel anxiety and still do a good job.

If there's nothing else you take from this book, let it be that truth.

Chapter Nine

A Stage Fright Land Mine

"Shame is a soul eating emotion."
— Carl Jung

If you've experienced speaker anxiety and stage fright sufficient to be reading this book, there's another dimension to the problem that I want to clue you into.

Shame.

Without exception, every person we've ever coached who labeled speaker anxiety as an issue also felt personal shame about it. Some aren't always aware of it at first. That Subby is a tricky thing, and for some people, shame is a sort of internal traffic cop that operates to keep you in line.

Shame and humiliation are emotions that psychologists and energy-based practitioners alike recognize are at the lowest rung of possible human emotion. In his insightful book *Power vs. Force,* David Hawkins says various emotions carry a vibration, and that shame is the lowest, hardest one to bear. Even anger and fear, he reasons, are of a higher vibration and closer to an optimal state of being than shame.

From an evolutionary biology perspective, you can see why Subby has such a good handle on doling out shame. In the age of hunter/ gatherers, our foraging ancestors were certainly as prone to negative behaviors as we are. Except back then, some behaviors were possibly more likely to result in death to the individual or tribe. Taking more than your share of food from the group threatened the whole. Betraying your family or tribe to another could have meant group annihilation. Sleep with the other guy's wife, or damage your neighbor's job—those things were a threat to the whole village, not just specific members of it. Short of death, shunning and enforced shame became the swiftest, most effective delivery method for jurisprudential punishment. Simply put, the capacity for shame could sometimes keep you and your community alive.

No wonder shame is so powerful. It's rigged right into the system, as strongly as the drives for hunger, thirst, sex, and novel information push us to eat, drink, procreate, and gossip.

Here's another insight we've observed to be true, related to shame: Anger is always the second emotion to occur inside a person. It usually comes right after another emotion that, for whatever reason, is too difficult or painful to feel. Shame, humiliation, powerlessness, impotence—those things are lower down on the rung of emotions.

Sometimes when a person is in a situation that does—or could— cause him to feel shame, he becomes angry. And feeling anger instead of the lower emotion is actually more positively energizing than being stuck in shame. It's preferable to feeling the *other thing*. And often the shift from shame to anger happens so fast that people miss the first and underlying emotion.

So perhaps now it makes more sense to you why sometimes you might have been angry at the colleague who kept insisting that you needed to address the meeting. Perhaps now you can feel why you're still mad at yourself for the missed slide, or the lost train of thought, or the way you hid in the office for months or years to avoid every potential speaking opportunity.

Feeling your anger was preferential to feeling the shame. But the shame is still in there, like a landmine, waiting to be triggered.

That's why, when we guide clients to clear their stage fright, we also guide them to clear the residual shame stored inside.

Sometimes the shame is tough to dislodge because it has its tentacles wrapped around so much of a person's constellation of memories and perspectives about him- or herself. Sometimes it's not hard to dislodge at all.

To dislodge shame, we use the same tools I described in Chapter Seven, as well as some guided imagery and other tools.

If you're up for it, I hope you will adjust your plans to do a little guided imagery work with me now. If you're reading this on a plane, or in some quiet place where you won't be interrupted, take the time not just to read the words that come next, but to sit with them enough to let them do the job they're intended to do. If you're in a more rambunctious setting, bookmark this section and come back to it. I promise you that it's completely worth doing.

Alternatively, there's an audio of my voice taking you through this and several other guided imagery exercises, that you can access on www.DissolveStageFrightNow.com/products.

Here we go.

Make yourself comfortable. Imagine that you're sitting in a beautiful setting—one that makes you feel relaxed and happy. If you're someone who prefers to be alone, be alone in this setting. If you're someone who prefers to be near people, imagine some nearby. If you want a pet there, put Fluff or Fido alongside you, but let's all understand that your pet is there to witness, not to interact with you.

When you have your setting, fill in the details. If you're at the beach, how warm is it? How far is the water from you? If you're in the woods, are you deep inside the trees or in a clearing? Fill in the details as completely as you can.

Now imagine that in front of you is something that looks like a shallow bowl. Notice that, in fact, that's exactly what it is. And with a gentle gust of breeze, the sand or the leaves or the dust or whatever's been hiding it blows away, and now you see it. Notice how the edges of it glimmer in the light. Notice how wide it is, and how deep. And now notice that it has the magic property to be able to hold endless amounts of anything, no matter what shape it looks to be.

That property makes it a very magical bowl. Imagine it filling up with a liquid that contains pure joy. There's a fountain or a faucet that appears out of nowhere, attached to nothing. And out of it is flowing this liquid peace. Notice that the bowl can just take in endless amounts of it. When you feel like you've filled it with enough of this wonderful elixir, notice that the fountain or the spigot just… stops running. No need for you to do a thing. It just knows to turn off, not because it runs out because there's an endless supply of this peaceful elixir. It just stopped because you decided there was enough for now.

Maybe now you swish your hand through the elixir. Maybe you sweep some out onto yourself, or you dip your face into it. Maybe you sip it. Maybe you simply see yourself reflected in the surface. What are you doing now? How are you interacting with it? Stay with this activity until it morphs into another, or it just simply comes to an end while you wait for the next thing to happen.

When you are ready, imagine that out of one of your index fingers, a little spigot suddenly materializes. It doesn't matter which finger, and it doesn't matter whether it's one or both. It doesn't hurt at all. It just is an opening, out of which something can pour and drain right out of you.

When you're ready, put your index finger into the magic liquid and let it rest there. It's easy to do—no strain at all. Notice that there's a slight pulling in your finger. And suddenly, as if by magic, there is something pouring out of your finger and into the magic elixir in the magic bowl. All the sources of shame in your body, whether you can feel them or not, are pooling into your finger and draining out of your finger, into the healing water. Stay here for as long as it takes just to let it all go.

All the shame for all the times you wanted to speak and didn't. All the times you spoke and it didn't work out the way you wished. All the times that spring to mind related to speaking. Or not speaking. Let it all drain away into the bowl.

When you feel like that's done, notice that your finger is repaired. It's suddenly just like a regular finger.

And notice how much lighter you feel, all over. You may be surprised and delighted to notice that your shoulders are looser. So is your neck. And your heart may feel larger, and more open.

Or you may feel nothing has changed. That's possible, too.

Here's the big thing to remember: There's nothing you ever did, whether or not you made a mistake, whether or not you made a miscalculation, whether or not you were ignorant of something, whether or not you made a gamble that didn't pay off—no matter what happened—nothing you did or didn't do is cause for feeling shame.

Whatever happened to you in the past, it happened. It happened, it's over, and you're okay anyway. You really are.

No one dies from public speaking. So the fact is, you will ALWAYS be okay anyway. Really.

Stepping Up For Your Self

Some of the most anxious people we know are also the bravest.

The irony is that living with speaker fear and stage fright is hard. It steals your sleep and your peace of mind. It can block everything from your peaceful sense of yourself to a project that would advance your career.

As hard as it is to live with, it can be easy to let go. It takes a moment of bravery, a leap of faith in a better future, to be able to get the help you need.

When you experience stage fright or speaker anxiety at any point along the spectrum, from feeling mildly uncomfortable to seriously scared, here's what it means:

Nothing.

It is not an indictment of your character.

It is not a weakness.

It is not a disaster waiting to happen.

It is not a Bad Sign.

It does not mean you are a loser.

It does not mean you can never get past it.

It does not mean you are doomed.

It does not mean people think you are weak or impotent.

It does not mean you will never be successful.

It does not mean you've let yourself down. Or that you've let anyone else down.

It does not mean you can never advance in your career.

It does not mean you *must* advance in your career.

It does not mean anything about *you*, as a person, *at all*.

It means you've had an experience or experiences that somehow make your subconscious mind believe your life is in danger when you step in front of a certain audience, or in front of any audience.

And it means you have an amygdala that's working brilliantly to keep you safe.

It means your subconscious doesn't have all the facts. When it gets more facts, your amygdala will be able to react in proportion and not shoot out the chemicals that you notice and experience as fear. Having speaker anxiety doesn't mean you can't be effective as a speaker. Whatever you're feeling is probably unnoticeable to us.

If it's so extreme that we do notice it, we will be rooting for you to do well, despite it.

It's completely possible to feel nervous and *still* do a credible to an excellent job of changing the audience. And remember: your job is *not* to do a good job. Your job is to help *us*—the audience—do a good job.

You can feel two things at once. And one of them can be nervousness. All you need is to feel the balance between the two—and be just a touch *more* confident than nervous, to stay on the beam. One thing that can tip the balance toward confidence is remembering that the point of your presentation is empowering us. We matter more than you do!

There are techniques to help you prevent the nervousness.

There are techniques to help you manage the nervousness.

There are techniques to help you succeed despite the nervousness. They are all easy to use, and easy to learn.

Finally, I want to point out that when you transform, others around you will need to shift, as well. When you become a more powerful and vocal advocate for your ideas and your Self, others will need to adjust their own patterns of thought and behavior as well. It will be true at work, and it may be true with family and close friends, as well.

Some around you will need nudging to see you in a new light. You'll need to step up for yourself by gently reminding people that you're no longer okay with hiding in your office and letting others do the talking. You'll have to assert your voice and ask to be put on the agenda, rather than waiting for others to notice the new you.

You may have colleagues who have enjoyed getting more than their share of the spotlight. They've become accustomed to you stepping back and ceding more visible leadership opportunities to them.

Some will be delighted to see how you've transformed...once they finally notice. Don't wait for them to notice. Don't get mad at them for not noticing. Be proactive and seize opportunities to own your spotlight.

Other colleagues may feel threatened by your transformation. They have a new normal to get acquainted with. The more you can create and deliver messages that make your listeners smarter, more insightful, better able to act, or empowered, the harder it will be to deny your voice.

Own your transformation. Don't back down to accommodate old patterns of behavior with the people around you. You've done too much work, and have too much at stake, to shrink yourself now.

Here's the rock bottom truth:

You have something to say that people want and need to hear. If you keep letting your brain chemistry run you, we won't get to hear it.

It's time to speak and lead. You're equal to it. You're ready for it. You were made for it. You wouldn't have been reading this book unless you were.

Take a chance. Try all the techniques we've set out here, and see what shifts. You'll be better for it. And so will the audiences who are waiting to hear from you.

If You Need More Help

Get it. Don't keep gutting this out alone. It hasn't worked so far, and it won't work now.

But if you find that you still have unacceptable levels of stage fright and speaker anxiety, let us help.

You can get a free handout to help you begin to understand the message behind your own stage fright by going to this URL: http:// invisiblelight.com/stage-fright.php

You can also request direct help.

InVisible Light has a process we use to help people put stage fright and speaker anxiety behind them so they can own the spotlight for their ideas and themselves.

The Own Your Spotlight Stage Fright D-Solver™ system has six parts:

1.   *Demystify the secret* behind stage fright
2.   *Decode the fear*
3.   *Deconstruct the messages* behind the fear
4.   *Dissolve* the triggers
5.   *Discover* the process to create a presentation with impact
6.   *Deliver your voice* and your message

If you're interested in our help, we'll give you a complementary strategy session to help you figure out what your next steps toward freedom might be. From there, we might recommend some group training, or one-on-one VIP coaching to help you dissolve stage fright. We may also recommend that you do nothing now, if you're not yet ready to move forward.

All around you, people are hiding in offices and cubicles, longing to be able to speak up but reluctant/afraid/terrified to do so. In meetings happening right now, there are people who have something to say, but they just…swallow it.

They tell themselves they'll put it in an email later. Meanwhile, your colleagues lose the present moment opportunity to hear about that idea, that strategy, that insight.

Don't let that be you.

All the good stuff is happening on the other side of your office door, out in the open. Don't let your best stuff be stuck on the wrong side of the door.

We see too many smart, discerning people stymied by speaker anxiety. The ideas they hold don't get heard and taken seriously.

Your voice is unique. Your perspectives are important. The more we can help people speak without fear, the better we all will be.

It's time to stop living in fear, and to raise your hand and your voice on behalf of the things that matter to you.

We need the difference your voice will make in the world!

Bonus
Chapter!

There's More To Stage Fright than You Think

On the next page begins a chapter of my upcoming book, *Performance Secrets Actors Know That Business Speakers Need to Steal.*

I'm including it here because this chapter deals with handling the unexpected. It's pretty common that scared speakers will fantasize about all the things that go wrong, so I wanted you to know some more about what to do if that happens.

More than that, I want you to see that you can learn to have calm nerves in the face of disaster—whether the disaster is a mind that goes blank or the electricity going out (and yes, I've seen both things happen in business meetings).

Actors know how to react appropriately in the moment because they're trained to be present. Staying present and focused on the prize, no matter what gets in your way, is your ticket to handling anything that happens no matter what the cause, so you can take care of the audience in your charge.

It takes knowing your script/presentation, and for that, we urge you to check out our book, *Speaking for Real*, our foolproof guide to creating a script for a presentation that works for your audience, your business, and yourself. You can find it on our website and on Amazon.

But even more than that, moving through speaker anxiety to a stronger, more grounded place takes a shift in perspective. And that's what I hope this bonus chapter gives you!

JUST SAY YES

In the theatre, the rules for improvisation are clear: Say "YES, and…" to everything.

That's why you'll never see improv actors say, "What do you mean we're on a cruise? We're on a safari!" Whatever happens first gets built upon next. An actor can say, "And aren't we lucky that this cruise goes through the African jungle, so we can see a giraffe from the deck!" But the actor can't negate what just happened.

Smart actors in scripted work also live by the "YES, and…" rule.

The chair tips over? Don't freeze and think, "THAT wasn't supposed to happen" and then miss your next cue. Don't avoid that side of the stage altogether, like you and the audience could just pretend together that the chair is still upright.

You say to yourself, "YES, that chair tipped over, and…" You go pick up the chair. Or you kick the chair. You sit on the fallen chair the way it lays. Good actors respond in character to the moment, exactly as it is. It's only a mistake if the actor makes it a big deal.

I've been on stage twice when a piece of set caught fire and a supremely composed actor (I'm looking at you Mitchell and Marty) put out the fire, in character, never missing a beat. I've been on stage when props dropped, characters failed to appear (I myself once failed to appear on cue—and I'm still sorry, Jerry), and entire scenes were jumped. We said, "Yes" and moved forward. By doing so, we took care of the audience AND the event we were there to perform.

In a performance of a play that used a massive turntable to shift scenes, we had a true catastrophe. A turntable is exactly what you recall from the last century—except instead of a record, it holds a platform, on which there is a set and furniture. It's an easy and fast way to shift scenery—you just spin the turntable around. One side, you're in the garden. One side, you're in the dining room.

On this particular night, the guys running the turntable put a little extra oomph into it to make the scene change faster and more dramatically. It was dramatic all right. Turntables can pick up centrifugal force. With the extra speed, the furniture spun off the turntable and lodged into the sides of the proscenium. As more furniture got stuck, the pieces began to break up with the force of being crushed. Amidst the sound of crashing and splintering wood, the turntable reached its limit of turn, with about half of each side of the set facing the audience.

Except there was more show to go on. So we climbed into the wreckage and somehow made it work. We made it work so well that the audience truly thought we did this every night. And the fifty or so people who were back for the second time (it was a fun show to see) knew they were watching something they'd never see again.

We just said, "YES, and..."

We even had mistakes happen in rehearsals that were so perfect that we figured out ways to repeat them. I once watched my friend Marty pound a metal garden table for effect, only to watch it collapse under his hand and scatter the bowl of berries it held. It was a brilliant metaphor for the state of his character, and immediately, the director (my husband, Jeffrey) asked the props people to find a way to rig it to fall on command. And every night, the divine mistake worked on cue. And every night, it made the audience gasp and see something true about the characters on stage.

What made these experiences fun instead of haunting was that most actors, at least by the point they get to be pros, are trained to stay calm, observe everything, take it in, and make an affirmative choice to move the action forward. They didn't stop the action to apologize to the audience. They said "Yes" to the moment and moved forward to the end.

Are there actors who beat themselves up afterwards when things go wrong? Sure. The difference is that they don't do it while the audience is watching.

Experienced actors go on stage with the clear goal to get through the performance from beginning to end, without stopping. They have a set of intentions to go after, and they're ready to say yes to any obstacles that arise, whether scripted or not, and chart a path around it. Whatever happens is perfect and was supposed to happen. And they do it all with the audience in mind.

Business speakers can take a page from this approach. Say, "YES, and…"
Don't be more committed to how things should look moment to moment than you are to whether or not the audience leaves better than when they walked in the room. Your job is to deliver a presentation that changes us in a deliberate way. We are there to become smarter, better able to understand and take an action. We aren't there to tell you that you did a good job of never saying, "Um."

Help yourself see the ultimate goal here: "Will they go away and put my ideas to work for them?" When you see the big picture, you lift your sights from the miniscule and mundane. You take our attention with you. So instead of all of us thinking about whether there's ketchup on your tie, or whether you just used the right acronym or not, we're thinking about how to use what you're sharing to make our own lives better somehow.

Saying "YES, and..." looks like this:

- If you get ahead or behind in the slides, just take a deep breath and go forwards or backwards.

- If you say something you didn't plan, just finish the thought and come back to what you *did* plan to say. Maybe you were picking up energy from the audience that made the impromptu moment perfect. Maybe you just had a brain fart. We won't care and we probably won't remember it.

- If your mind draws a blank—actors call it "going up" because often the person's eyes will look up, as if she could read the right lines off a screen in her forehead—just say to yourself, "YES." I mean that literally. Saying an internal yes, and with a smile if you can manage it, will almost always unlock your brain and let you think again.

- Remember that no one in the room knows what you planned to say or do. So no one will miss anything you skip. Let it go.

- If you spill the water, you spill the water. Someone will help you clean it up. Keep talking. Use a water bottle with a cap and the worst you can do is knock it over.

- If something goes haywire, absorb it the way you would if you were in a small group. So you sneezed. So someone asked a question you didn't expect. So you said, "Um." You don't panic in your living room. Don't let that small moment interfere with making sure we, in the audience, see the big picture.

At InVisible Light, we've seen a speaker we coached speak through a fire alarm and sprinklers going off. (He nailed his "Big Idea" and then organized the evacuation.) We've seen speakers succeed in connecting to the audience in spite of scenery falling over, slides and electricity failing, the teleprompter going down, a sick audience member, or being sick themselves.

In every case, our speakers took in the circumstances, reacted to them, and took care of the audience either by continuing to talk, summoning help, making their biggest points, or ending the talk in a way that took care of the audience. They said, "YES, that happened, AND..."

Which brings us to a key sub-rule of saying "YES, and..."

No apologizing.

Don't tell us that you planned to speak for forty-five minutes, but you were told just before you went on that you only have thirty. If you know what matters in your talk, you can give it to us in thirty minutes. We want your content—not the time. And most audiences would be thrilled to get it in thirty minutes instead of forty-five.

No apologies. No justification. No complaints. No whining.

Speakers use those devices to try to take themselves off the hook:

- "Well, they told me we were running out of time, so I'm going to skip my opening remarks and just jump to slide ten." (big sigh)

- "We're out of time, but I have a lot of slides left, so catch me later and I'll tell you more then." (breathless speech)
- "Okay, well, we're just going to skip these slides here. I really like them, but I can't show them." (whine whine whine)

You've heard all those excuses, haven't you? Maybe you've even spoken some yourself.

But in trying to make themselves feel better, these speakers make *us* in the audience feel bad. Do we take your side against the previous speaker who went over and cost you time? Do we feel sorry for you? More likely, we feel sorry for ourselves. No matter what you have to say, we're left wondering whether the really *good* part was skipped. Unless we're happy you skipped something. If you can actually skip the opening remarks and leap to slide ten, maybe we should be *glad* you didn't subject us to something so evidently useless. Why did we sit in the room to hear you speak for thirty minutes if you can't take us to the conclusion, and you're making us chase you down in the hall to get it?

And it doesn't make the speaker actually feel better anyway. All it does is focus his attention on what can no longer happen—the presentation going the way he envisioned it. But if he can just say, "YES, and…" he can in THIS MOMENT still have an impact on the audience that can make the audience grateful to have been in the room to hear.

If the slides go out, we'll all notice that. And we'll panic with you, if you go there. We'll be okay with it if you just say "YES, and…" move on.

You don't have to apologize to us for the failure. We get it. We have eyes. Just move on. If you know your major points well enough, you won't need slides to launch them to us. And if you DON'T know your major points that well, you aren't ready to speak to us anyway.

There's another category of common speaker apology that falls into the realm of, "I'm not as prepared as I wish, so please don't judge me." The No Apologies rule applies there, too—but for different reasons, that we'll look at in Chapter 5.

We leave you with this true story.

We once saw a speaker address an audience of thousands, in his first big presentation as the CEO of this company. Fresh from a rival company, he had been joking around for days, saying, "I hope I don't call them by [the old company's name]! Hahaha!"

And then he did it, for real.

In front of the new company, he said, "It's great to be here with the owners and operators of [the old company name.]"

But he was awake enough to hear himself do it, and the next words out of his mouth weren't an apology. He reached for something so much better. "I'll never say those words again. From now on, I get to say, 'It's great to be here with the owners and operators of [the new company.]' And I couldn't be happier."

If he could live through THAT without apologizing, so can you. Be awake.

No apologizing.

Just say YES, and…

These are ideas to steal.

The next idea to steal springs directly from that last story: What you rehearse shows up on stage. No apologizing.
Just say YES, and…
These are ideas to steal.

The next idea to steal springs directly from that last story: What you rehearse shows up on stage.

About
Jane Beard

Jane Beard is on a mission to help timid speakers find something to say, finally face a crowd, and make the impact they want to make.

Jane was an award-winning, professional actor for many years. She appeared in plays around the country, voiced commercials, appeared on camera in commercials, and appeared in feature films and television. From her work creating, rehearsing and performing roles, she learned skills she shares with high-level business presenters today:

- How to take an audience on a memorable journey with a beginning, middle, and end—whether the journey is through Chekov's *Uncle Vanya*, or the Plan of Action for the coming fiscal year

- How to rehearse in a way that allows you to deliver a performance that feels fresh, immediate, and authentic every time

- What can get in the way of an audience connecting to a speaker/performer, and what can break down barriers to deeper audience connection

- How to get a laugh when you want one, and

- The one thing everyone in the audience wants, each time he or she is in an audience.

Jane is a sought-after speaker, and radio and television guest. She's the author of *Speaking for Real: A Foolproof Guide to Bold, Authentic Presentations*, and *15 Things to FORGET Before Your Next Presentation.*

She is President of InVisible Light. InVisible Light helps senior executives create and deliver presentations that change the trajectory of companies and careers.

She lives in Silver Spring, Maryland, with her husband and InVisible Light business partner, Jeff Davis. She enjoys gardening and anything related to baseball, but especially the Washington Nationals.

You may contact Jane at JaneBeard@InVisibleLight.com. Learn more at www.InVisibleLight.com.

Made in the USA
Middletown, DE
04 February 2024

49095076R00070